Walking with God

Walking with God

DERICK BINGHAM

AMBASSADOR

Belfast Northern Ireland Greenville South Carolina

Walking with God
© Copyright 2000 Derick Bingham

ISBN 1 84030 084 1

AMBASSADOR PUBLICATIONS
a division of
Ambassador Productions Ltd.
Providence House
Ardenlee Street,
Belfast,
BT6 8QJ
Northern Ireland
www.ambassador-productions.com

Emerald House
427 Wade Hampton Blvd.
Greenville
SC 29609, USA
www.emeraldhouse.com

Introduction

You meet them all over the world. They are people who were once keen, contented, bright Christians, but, somehow, along the line they grew cold in heart, weary in spirit, bitter of temperament, and now follow their Lord at a distance. Like Demas, Paul's partner and companion, who fell in love with 'this present age', they have not lost their souls, but, they have left the track.

This book looks at subjects like BACKSLIDING - its causes and cure; GUIDANCE - with instructions to heed, limits to observe and examples to follow; SUFFERING - and the inexplicable silence of God; WORRY - and seeks to give a biblical answer to the king of all addictions, and, VALUES - things worth standing up for and God's standards in worship and behaviour.

May God use this series of studies to the reader as together we walk with God through life's labyrinth of ways.

Contents

Worry

A BIBILCAL ANSWER TO THE
KING OF ALL ADDICTIONS

A lady was tossing and turning in her bed one evening. She was worried about her son who had just recently got married. "Why are you worried about him?", said her husband, "He has married a perfectly nice girl who will look after him. Just what are you worried about?"."Oh", she said as she turned yet again in her bed, "I'd be worried if I wasn't worried".

The lady represents a lot of people. Day after day, millions of people waste precious energy and even more precious time focussing their minds on things they have no business trying to deal with or solve or worrying about things that will, in fact, never happen. They charge about with stomachs like spindryers with worry gnawing away in their minds cutting their lifeline to joy and staunching their creativity.

The Bible has a very clear answer to worry. In fact it teaches that worry is a sin, it is a lack of trust in God and His promises. God would have us without anxious care and in this study we want to look at God's way of de-programming the worrier. Is there something over-whelming you at this time? Is there something, bitter as gall, turning you into a frantic individual and stealing your balance in life? Is worry increasing tension in your life to a dangerous level? Here is the Biblical answer to the king of all addictions. May you learn to kick the habit before it kicks you into misery, unhappiness and depression. There is, thank God, a cure available. I trust this short study will help you to apply it.

I. PLENTY TO WORRY ABOUT

Everything today is changing very fast. Computer companies have no sooner put out a new product than they are keeping an even newer one under wraps so that they can sell their present product. We are living in what has been called the "Three Minute Culture". Television advertising tries to sell you as many as four products in three minutes. Twenty years ago, a trade representative on the road wouldn't have dreamt of trying to sell the General Store proprietor four products in three minutes. He would have gone to see him, had a coffee with him, asked him about his family, chatted about a dozen and one things before even getting around to the mere mentioning of his product. Now it's all down to three minutes and the product will sell, not necessarily on its quality, but on the cleverness of its advertising. Cleverness is all.

In the midst of all the hectic pace of modern life, the addiction of worry arises. Under pressure of advertising, people worry that they haven't "made it". Young people worry that they haven't got the right image. The big question of the hour is "are you busy?" If you aren't glancing at your watch to rush on to the next thing, you aren't really living! If you are quietly eating an apple at the side of the street at 3 o'clock in the afternoon, people are inclined to think there is something wrong with you! They almost want you to feel guilty.

Of course frantic living is not the only cause of worry for many people. Unemployment is the other side of the coin. Studies have shown that many people who lose their jobs go through a period of depression. Some get into a vicious circle of declining self-respect, money worries and boredom and they become chronically pessimistic. Reaction to loss of a job is similar to other major losses in life such as the loss of a limb or the death of a loved one. Other worries plague people. All around us there are people facing a broken relationship, or a failed exam, or the frustration of plans foiled by unexpected circumstances. Society around us is drifting into moral chaos and that brings its worries. Old and trusted values are falling. Belief in God is under attack. As E. F. Schumacher has said, "When there are so many gods all competing with one another and claiming first priority and there is no supreme God, no supreme good or value, in terms of which everything else needs to justify itself, society cannot but drift into chaos."[1]

As we look at politics, or the judiciary, or industry or business and commerce, moral values are often swamped with vested interest and people's downright selfishness and ambition. There is a cynicism abroad which would cause anyone to worry. The rise of the occult is also a cause of worry and it has been pointed out that it would probably be safe to say that there are now more witches in England and America than at any time since the Reformation.

And what can we say about the New Age Movement sweeping into Western culture? It is full of pantheism which teaches that there is no distinction between the Creator and His creation. Everything, animate and inanimate is part of a single, impersonal energy called God. "There is", writes Shirley McLaine, the actress, "one basic spiritual law which would make the world a happier and healthier place and it is that everyone is God - everyone". Shirley even takes upon herself the Divine title, "I know that I exist, therefore I am. I know that God exists, therefore it is. But since I am part of that force I am that I am". Such fundamental ego-centricity is blasphemous. It puts the self in the place of God and even declares we are God. New Agers have succumbed to the temptation Satan put to Adam and Eve in the Garden; "You shall be as gods". All around us we see the rise of belief and reincarnation. It also sees Shamanism, which is the art of controlling the spirit world using dreams, visions and "learning to fly within ourselves".

We see the rise of Silva Mind Control which is the transformation of the mind to gain expertise in problem solving involving out-of-body projection during hypnosis. We see Suggestology which is accelerated learning, an accelerated learning method originating in Bulgaria using music and rhythmic breathing. We see Visualisation which is imagining something which one desires in order to achieve it, i.e. changing reality by mental projection. We even have Biofeedback which is the technique of controlling normally involuntary bodily functions such as heart-beat or blood pressures to attain a higher awareness of states of consciousness on a scale of 1 (deep sleep) to 8 (cosmic consciousness). Astrologers are on the rise and people are starting to live by what their "stars" say. Such trends are worrying, to say the least.

As we look across the international scene with its wars, its terrorism, its atrocities, its drug trafficking and fraud on a mind-boggling scale, who does not feel worry and fear for the future gripping the mind? What with famines and earthquakes, floods and tornadoes, disasters of all kinds, is there a place where worry can be swopped for inner peace, no matter what the circumstances? Is there a state of equanimity which can face any disturbance? There certainly is and you can find it.

2. WHY WORRY WHEN YOU CAN TRUST?

The scene is a Sunday afternoon in Northern Ireland and quite a stir is being caused. From England and Scotland and from various parts in the Province itself, dozens of people are beginning to converge on the tiny Copeland Islands just off the Northern Ireland coastline. The cause of their interest has not been seen for a hundred and eight years and everyone is determined to, at least, get a glance at it.

What has happened? A white thrush from Russia on a migrating track for Australia has, it seems, been blown off course. Local ornithologists are ecstatic at seeing such a rare appearance in their own back yard.

The greatest teacher who ever lived would certainly not ask us to wait for the rare appearances of foreign birds on our shores before we study our feathered friends. He teaches us that we should constantly consider the birds of the air, if only to learn from them to trust our Heavenly Father and not to have worry-filled lives.

"Therefore I say to you, do not worry about your life, what you will eat or what you will drink; nor about your body, what you will put on. Is not life more than food and the body more than clothing? Look at the birds of the air for they neither sow nor reap nor gather into barns; yet your Heavenly Father feeds them. Are you not of more value than they?" says the Lord Jesus. (Matt. 6: 25-26).

What is Christ saying here about the subject of worry? He is saying that most people are pre-occupied with a trinity of cares; they are primarily concerned with what they will eat, with what they will drink and with what they will wear. People are primarily concerned with the welfare of their bodies. If you doubt Christ's teaching, just lift the nearest magazine or newspaper and have a look at the advertisements. Alternatively, study today's television advertising. What is the theme of these advertisements? Every one of them is primarily concerned with the welfare of the body. They concentrate on how to feed it, rest it, refresh it, clothe it, entertain it, or titillate it. There is the next exciting novel to read, the present in-place to holiday, the best airline to get you there, the smartest car to drive or the most potent perfume to buy. Here is a page advertising beautiful jewellery or shoes, or whatever, to be an accessory to the best clothes you step out in. The body, though, is the object to which all these advertisements are related. Take the human body away, it seems, and there would be nothing to advertise!

If your body and its comforts is all you are interested in, then Christ is saying yours is a false view of what human beings and human life is all about. If food, clothes and drink is all you are living for, you will get, in going after them, all the worry you can ever hope for, and a lot of ulcers to boot.

You still doubt it? Think then of some young person who has, unfortunately, been recently paralysed or badly hurt in some accident. They will never walk again, or see again, or even move out of bed in their own strength. They cannot even lift a book to read. Now they turn to you and say, "What is life all about?" You say, "Having a good time". They can't move to have one. "Life is eating lovely food", you answer. They have to get others to feed them. "Life is having wonderful holidays", you suggest. They aren't going anywhere.

"Life is going to see exciting films". They have been blinded.

"Money", you say in desperation, "is the thing to live for". It might buy them a better bed, but is life a better bed?

Physical well-being is not a worthy object for a lifetime's devotion. You are not big enough to be the object of your life. There has got to be more to life or else the longings within us are a mockery. Those who are Christ's disciples know very well that food, drink and clothes, or a preoccupation with them, is not the supreme goal in life.

The realist, of course, thinks that Christ's teaching is unrealistic. They think Christ is forbidding human beings to use their minds or to plan for the future. If they would consider again His teaching about the birds of the air, they would be aware that He is doing no such thing. What, after all, was our friend, the Russian white thrush doing when it got blown off course to Northern Ireland? Migrating.

No creature plans for the future more than birds do. "Consider them", says Christ. He is not banning human beings from using their minds to prepare for the future. He is not banning thought or forethought, but He is banning anxious thought. Distracting, self-tormenting, corroding, throttling worry is a sin for a Christian.

Christ's argument in this matter is devastatingly logical. "Is not life more than food and the body more than clothing", He argues. Put it this way; were you frightened and worried that you might not live to read the end of this chapter? Of course you weren't. You trusted God to give you life to breathe. In fact you never even think about it, do you? You always trust Him for it. Well then, if you don't worry about God giving you life every second, why then are you worried all the time about what you're going to eat, about what you're going to drink and about what you're going to wear?

Of course the realists will say that we can't expect God to drop food and clothes and drink from Heaven to us; we have to work for them. So do the birds He asks us to consider. They don't sow and gather harvests into barns like farmers, but they work very hard. God does not feed them in the immediate sense, they actually feed themselves. Some eat seeds, some eat fish, some eat insects, some are predators and others scavenge. God provides in nature all they need to feed themselves. But they are without anxious care about it.

God does the same thing for us. There are ample sources in the earth and sea for everyone. The sad thing is that the selfishness of mankind means that sources are often wasted, or hoarded or spoiled. God has provided for our needs and we need to get out there and work to have them in adequate supply for our homes and families and to help with the needs of others. But we should be like the birds and do it without worry.

And what about plants? Even Solomon in all his glory was not clothed like the lilies of the field, Christ taught. The lilies don't toil like men in a field or spin like women in the house, but they have to draw sustenance from the sun and soil. If God clothes the grass you walk on so wonderfully, which is here today and gone tomorrow, will He not do the same for you? "Oh you of little faith!" says Christ.

Do not for a moment imagine that Christ is saying that His people will not experience trouble. God clothed the grass but it is cut down. God protects sparrows, but they have accidents, can face overexposure to the cold and they do die, sometimes, of diseases. So it is with people. Wars overwhelm us, accidents strike us in seconds, diseases waste our bodies, trouble erupts in our workplace, unemployment strikes at our pay-packets. It is a fact that God permits suffering. The cross up ahead of the One who taught the truths we are now studying, was going to present suffering above all suffering. Christ did not promise freedom from responsibility, freedom from unexpected circumstances, freedom from complications that baffle, but He categorically promised freedom from worry. All who trust Him can know it.

"Which of you by worrying can add one cubit to his stature?", said the Saviour. The king of all addictions is totally unproductive. Worry won't cure your problems, won't lift and inspire your heart, won't make you easier to live with or won't help those who come across your path. Even worry about tomorrow will make no difference to tomorrow. Today has been given to us and we should get on with what God demands of us today. When tomorrow comes, there will be new troubles, but also renewed strength to face them. There is a touch of humour in the Saviour's advice, is there not, that we should let tomorrow worry about its own things? Today has enough trouble and enough strength from God to get through it.

So it is that feverish worry "amounts to idolatry for its accompanying attachment to mammon means detachment from God. It blurs vision, for, by being preoccupied with piling up material wealth, it obscures the real goal of our existence, it confuses values, for it attaches primary significance to that which is secondary, and vice-versa as if food were more important than life and clothing than the body. It defies all reason for it barters away heavenly for earthly treasures, the imperishable for the perishable, forgets that it cannot even add one cubit to a person's life-span; borrows tomorrow's troubles as if today's were inadequate; and, worst of all, refuses to consider that if, even as Creator, God feeds the birds and clothes the lilies, then certainly, as Heavenly Father, He will care for His children". [2]

What, then is the alternative to worry? The alternative is to trust the Lord and to be preoccupied with seeking to put His kingdom and His righteousness first in our lives. In our home, in our schooling or university of higher education, in our marriage, in our business, in our professional life, in our part as citizens of the state, in our tax returns or whatever, we must seek to put God and His interests first. God's kingdom exists where Jesus Christ is consciously acknowledged. We must seek at all times to extend that kingdom and if we do, God will take care of our material needs. Having a God-centred life is having a worry-free life;

having a self-centred life is to have a worry-packed life. The choice is ours.

It is always good to earth spiritual teaching, as the Saviour did, by practical example. There is a superb example of practical outworking of what Christ is teaching about worry which we can take from the life of that incorrigible Cornish miner and preacher, Billy Bray. Let him tell about the incident himself and may his example inspire us into worry-free living.

Billy was always building new little chapels all over Cornwall and Devon for the worship of God and for the preaching of the Gospel. Billy was very famous for his wit and eccentric sayings and his deep and fervent love for the Lord was respected by many thousands of people. His faith was a very practical faith and in this particular incident concerning the chapel at Kerley Downs, his faith and trust in God truly shines. F. W. Bourne in his book "Glory", a compelling biography of Billy Bray, describes the incident. "When the little place at Kerley Downs was up, Billy began to think where the pulpit could come from. At last, as he looked about among some furniture at an auction sale, his eye fell upon an old three- cornered cupboard. "The very thing!" cried Billy, "The very thing. I can cut a slit down the back of un, and strengthen the middle of un, and put a board up in front of un, and clap a pair o' steers behind un, and then the preacher can preach out of un pretty".

With much glee he turned to someone near him, and asked, 'What do 'e think they'll want for that there cupboard?' The man looked and gave it is as his opinion that it would go for six shillings. Billy told him what he meant to do with it, and the man said - 'Why, you're Billy Bray. Here, I'll give 'e the six shilling to buy it'.

After a while the cupboard was put up. Billy knew nothing of auctions. All eager to have his pulpit, he cried, holding out his hand - 'Here Mister Auctioneer, here's six shillin' for un; I do want un for a pulpit'. Of course there was a great laugh at Billy's expense. As it passed away the auctioneer cried - 'Six shillings, going for six'. A nod from behind Billy was quickly caught. 'Seven,' said the auctioneer, 'seven shillings.'

'No,' cried Billy, ''tis only six; there's the money.' Of course, down went the hammer and much to Billy's astonishment, the cupboard was not his.

'Well, Father do know best,' said he in a rather disappointed tone; but anyhow I must give the man back his six shilling.'

The man was gone, nor was Billy likely to see him again. This was a new and even greater trouble.

'I'll be gone down and tell Father about it,' said Billy, as he started off for his little chapel.

With faith renewed, and a comfortable assurance that it would be all right, he was coming from the chapel, when he saw the cupboard going up the hill in a cart. 'I'll follow un, anyhow,' he whispered, 'an' see the end.' They carried it to a house, and tried to take it inside, but it was just too big to get in. They twisted and turned, they pulled and pushed, but it was no use.

'Here's a mess,' said the purchaser angrily; 'I've given seven shilling for un, an' shall have to skat un up for firewood.'

Then, as his eyes twinkled, Billy stepped over and put his hand on the man's shoulder as he stood, hat in hand, wiping his forehead. 'I'll give 'e six shillin' for un, if you'll carry un down to my little chapel.'

'That I will,' said the man, pleased at being so well out of it.

'Bless the Lord!' cried Billy, 'it's just like Him, He knew I couldn't carry un myself, so He got this man to carry un for me.' [3]

3. WHY WORRY WHEN YOU CAN PRAY?

The scene is Philippi in Macedonia, famed scene of the decisive battle in which armies loyal to the murdered Julius Caesar, fighting under the joint command of Octavian and Mark Anthony, defeated the rebel forces of Brutus and Cassuis. Now enlarged, the city, named after the father of Alexander The Great, has been given the "Ius Italicum" which represents the legal quality of Roman territory in Italy - the highest privilege obtainable by a provincial municipality. Philippi is a colony of Rome and its people could purchase and own or transfer property and have the right to civil law suits. They are exempt from both the poll tax and are proud of it.

The Gospel of Jesus Christ slips into the city of Philippi in ever so quiet a fashion. The Gospel also slips on to the Continent of Europe for the first time. It is interesting to note that the first sermon preached is given, not standing up, but sitting down. No fanfare or public relations experts preceded it, no advertising campaign makes the people aware of the life-changing nature of what is about to invade their lives and cultures. Paul, the great Christian Apostle, in Philippi for the first time, finds some Jewish women holding a prayer meeting down on a river bank. He sits down among them and speaks of Christ. A business woman called Lydia has a conversion experience as he talks. "The Lord", says Scripture, "opened her heart". Lydia then opens her home to the Apostle and his friends, Timothy, Silas and Luke, and the Lord opens Philippi and a Continent to His Gospel.

It is fascinating to meditate on the fact that Lydia's heart was God's highway to Europe. Soon a Philippian jailer is converted in earthquake circumstances and a Christian Church begins to meet in Lydia's home.

One memorable day, a letter arrives for the young Church at Philippi, written by Paul. Of all the letters he wrote, this is to prove to be, unquestionably, the happiest. It may have been written for more or less personal reasons, but inspired of the Holy Spirit, everything in it has a universal application, even to our circumstances today. The laws of the spiritual life never change. This is why the advice given in this amazing letter is as applicable today as it was when it was first written. This is why the Bible is of such vital importance in the life of the christian; every conceivable experience which the christian may have to face has already been met and dealt with somewhere in the Scriptures. Here then is an astonishing and remarkable letter.

This theme of the Philippian letter is a very contagious subject. Sixteen times the word "joy" and its derivitive "rejoice" is mentioned. Victory in Christ is bringing joy to Paul's life like nothing else ever has. He writes that the One who has begun a good work in the Philippian christian's lives will finish it. Mankind might leave unfinished temples and abandoned projects. Artists may leave unfinished pictures, entrepreneurs may leave unfinished business plans but the One who creates a desire for God in us, reveals the work of Christ and the real meaning of Calvary to us, forgives our sins and creates new life in us, goes on to make us more like Christ through all the circumstances of life.

Paul underlines the fact that he will go on doing it "until the day of Jesus Christ" (Philippians 1; 6). What does this mean? It means that until the day when there will be "a new heaven and a new earth in which righteousness dwells" and Christ will return to reign as King, God will continue to work in a christian's life knocking off the rough edges and making us more like the Lord Jesus. It is a formidable task. "How on earth do you do it?", said someone to the sculptor as he faced a huge block of marble out of which he had to carve a horse. "Everything that does not look like a horse has to go!", he replied quietly.

So it is that everything that is not Christlike in the believer's life has to go: that is God's continual aim as He works in a christian's life. This confidence in God's continuing work in the life of the christian is the basis of Paul's incorrigible joy. Joy, you see, is not a feeling so much as it is an attitude.

It is an equanimity of spirit which is not determined by people, or circumstances, or possessions or lack of them. With most people, if their circumstances are overwhelming, they too are in chaos of mind and spirit. Not Paul. He writes to the Philippian christians while under house arrest, quite possibly chained to a soldier on either wrist, and certainly with no privacy from dawn to dusk, from the midnight hour to the cock crowing.

The man who writes of joy and contentment is facing trial before a notorious Emperor called Nero who might have him beheaded at any time. Yet, he is at peace!

If you think your circumstances are bad; try these. "From the Jews five times I received forty stripes minus one. Three times I was beaten with rods; once I was stoned; three times I was shipwrecked; a night and a day I have been in the deep. In journeys often, in perils of waters, in perils of robbers, in perils of my own countrymen, in perils of the Gentiles, in perils in the city, in perils in the wilderness, in perils in the sea, in perils among false brethren; in weariness and toil, in sleeplessness often, in hunger and thirst, in fastings often, in cold and nakedness - besides the other things, what comes upon me daily, my deep concern for all the churches". (2 Corinthians 11; 24-28). It is quite obvious that lashings cannot beat the joy out of Paul's life, weary travelling in wilderness country cannot dry up his joy, false christians cannot poison his joy, cold weather and exposure cannot freeze it, and burning sun cannot wither it.

These are not the musings of some ivory tower sophisticate who doesn't live in the nitty gritty of life; this is a man who speaks truth right out of the cauldron of reality. There is in his life a distinct absence of the things that make life comfortable, yet Paul doesn't lose his joy. He doesn't moan, "Why does God allow these things?", nor does he become soured and embittered and turn his back upon Christ and His Church. He is confident, even though a victim. He is joyful, in spite of others. He is hopeful, regardless of uncertainty. He is contented because Christ is central to his life. For him to live is Christ and to die is more of Christ.

Why is he, though, not eaten up with worry? Couldn't he be allowed to worry, just a little? With everything seemingly against him, how could this man survive with such a calm, contented spirit? How can any christian survive without worry? Paul lets the Philippians know his secret and his secret can be ours. He puts it in one incredible sentence.

"Be anxious for nothing", he writes, "but in everything by prayer and supplication with thanksgiving, let your requests be made known to God and the peace of God which surpasses all understanding will guard your heart and mind through Christ Jesus". (Philippians 4; 6-7). In this simple, powerful sentence lies the cure to the king of all addictions. In the light of it, if applied to your life, it will make worry flee.

What is worry? It is, according to the dictionary, "to be unduly concerned". It comes from the German word "wurgen" which means "to strangle, to choke". Worry very quickly becomes the dictator of how you feel and react to your circumstances, mentally harassing you, emotionally stringing you out and spiritually strangling you. A worry can be defined as anything that drains your life of joy. What then is Paul telling us in Philippians 4; 6-9? He is saying, "Worry about nothing and pray about everything". He is saying to all of us, "Switch everything from your worry list to your prayer list". He is calling us to let God know what is troubling us. He is saying, in effect, that prayer is a conversation with, a plea directed to, a request made of, information given to the supreme Person of the Universe who can hear, know, understand, care about and respond to the concerns that otherwise would sink us in despair.

But notice that the real accent of this amazing sentence of Paul's is that prayer is to be given with thanksgiving. As Barth put it, "To begin by praising God for the fact that in this situation, as it is, He is so mightily God - such a beginning is the end of anxiety. To be anxious means that we ourselves suffer, ourselves groan, ourselves seek to see ahead. Thanksgiving means that giving God the glory in everything, making room for Him, casting our care upon Him, letting it be His care.

The troubles that exercise us then cease to be hidden and bottled up. They are, so to speak, laid open to God, spread out before Him".

If we do this, what ensues? The peace of God will be ours. The expression, "The peace of God" found here is found nowhere else in the New Testament. It isn't peace with God, that we have already when we are justified by faith in Christ, such peace is pre-supposed. It is the tranquility of God's own eternal being, the peace which God Himself has - the calm serenity that characterises God's very nature and which christians are welcome to share. This peace of God will, according to Scripture, pass all understanding. What does this mean? It means it is able to produce better results than human planning. It is far superior to any person's schemes for security. It is more effective for removing anxiety than any intellectual effort or power of reasoning.

Think about this. If you were to gather every brilliant mind from the universities of your country, from the Government of your country, from the schools of your country and set them to solve the particular problem which is worrying you today, prayer will bring a peace in your circumstances which will far surpass all that these minds could come up with! It "rises above" all understanding.

There are certain questions we have in life which are not answered for us. Like Job, we do not know why we are going through certain alarming difficulties in our lives, but God, although He has not explained the situation, has promised us that He will give us sufficient grace to enable us to go through. It is part of our discipline sometimes to be kept in ignorance to be shown that we are finite and the important thing is not so much what happens to us as our attitude to what happens. Prayer transforms our attitude and immediately we start praying, a calm confidence and the experience of the peace of God will supplant worry and anxiety. Scripture promises that as a result of prayer, God's peace will flood your life. Try it; it beats worry, any day. As for the nightime, just hand those worries to God in prayer before you go to bed tonight. Why? Because He is going to be up all night anyway, isn't He?

4. WHY WORRY WHEN YOU HAVE A GUIDE?

I had a question for him. His name was Mr. Neville Taylor, decorated by the French Government for, among other things, his very dedicated work of translating the Scriptures into the Mbai language of the Tchad.

"How did you translate the verse in Isaiah 26; 3?" I asked him. It is a verse which speaks of how a person is kept in perfect peace whose mind is stayed on God. "We translated it that God would keep the person's heart 'lying down' whose mind was stayed on Him," Neville answered. My mother was dying and coming home from school-teaching one day, I remember very well laying my books down at the bottom of her bed and looking her straight in the eye and, loving her very much, I gently asked what it meant to be a Christian when one had to go through what my dear mother was suffering. "Do you see that text on the wall?", she said. It read, "Thou will keep him in perfect peace whose mind is stayed on Thee". "I had a friend", she said, "who was a missionary in China and the local dialect which she spoke had that verse say, "Thou will keep him in perfect peace whose mind stops at God".

I love those two stories of two translations of Isaiah's famous verse because they perfectly sum up all that God does for the worried mind that rests on Him. The Scriptures are actually calling us to take our minds beyond the immediate worry of our lives and rest them on the God of our lives. So, don't let your mind stop at your worry; let it stop at God. It really does make a difference. It will result in a heart that, as the Mbai folk would say, "lies down".

As you let your mind stop at God, then His character and attributes become more and more relevant to you. One of those great attributes is that God is our Guide. "He leads me beside the still waters...... He leads me in the paths of righteousness for His Name's sake", writes King David. What does that mean? It means that if God does not guide you, then His very Name and its worth are at stake. How many advertisements do you see in modern life with the phrase attached, "and that's guaranteed"? God's Name, reverently speaking, is His guarantee. He is not on probation, either, nor does He have to pass an examination. His Name is to be trusted, not put on probation.

There is no greater cure for worry than the promise of the guidance of God. It is not, though, that it is always easy to understand, is it?

Let's think about three incidents in Scripture on the subject of the guidance of God for our help.

Take the disciples on the lake, for example. It is dark and "Jesus was not come to them" (John 6; 17). Their little vessel is plunging and lunging in a heavy storm and they have rowed for over three hours and have only covered about three miles. Where is their Master? At a prayer meeting with His Father on a mountain. There is no sign of Him coming to the aid of His worried and frightened disciples. Where is the God who promises to lead them, now?

The second example concerns a very cultured character called Jairus. With great courage he has identified with Christ by falling at His feet and pleading with Him to come and help his dying daughter. Jesus turns to go with Him but as He passes through the crowd, an anonymous woman touches the fringe of His robe. Our Lord not only takes time to hear some of the thronging people deny having touched Him, He takes time to wait for the woman to confess to it. There is no sense of hurry as He stays to pronounce a blessing upon her in the hearing of the crowd. While Jesus lingers, speaking to the woman, messengers come from the house of the synagogue ruler to say that any further appeal to Jesus is of no use; his little daughter has died. Can you imagine how Jairus felt in that circumstance? What is the Lord, who leads and guides His people, doing with him now? The delay of the Lord Jesus must have seemed extremely strange.

The third case concerns Christ's closest friends, Mary, Martha and Lazarus. One might, outwardly, have seen the reason why Jesus delayed in going to help the storm-tossed disciples (prayer) or Jairus' daughter (a fellow sufferer) but the delay in visiting his very sick friend Lazarus was deliberate (See John 11: 5-7). Then, when Lazarus died, the Lord took His time, deliberately, on the journey to Bethany. How do we know? The answer is very straightforward. From Betharba where Christ was at the time, to Bethany where Lazarus lived, was about two days distance by foot; so, the Lord could easily have got to Bethany before Lazarus' illness had given place to death. Even, after that, He evidently lingered on the journey for when He reached Bethany, the Bible tells us that Lazarus had already been four days in the tomb! Friend and all as Christ was to Mary, Martha and Lazarus, deliberate delay in coming to their aid seems incredibly strange.

Was God guiding in all these delays? Of course. He delayed with the disciples in the storm because he wanted to teach them that He had power over nature. He came, in His perfect timing and calmed the waters. He delayed to visit Jairus' daughter to prove to Jairus that He not only had power over disease. He also had power over death. Mary and Martha both scolded Christ for not being at hand on time; they both said on separate occasions, "Lord, if you had been here, my brother would not have died". Imagine scolding the One who has never allowed a planet to be late yet, never mind Himself!

Christ, of course, delayed in order to show them, among other things, that not only had He power over nature or death, He had power over decomposition. Christ raised the already decomposing body of Lazarus from the tomb. His delays always become His delights.

We must never worry when God delays to resolve a situation. All things that happen to us are not good but they work together for good. Always. He will not leave you guideless, Christian. You are no longer lost, you have been found by the Good Shepherd and He is always leading you on to further and better things.

Did Joseph think God was guiding when he was thrown into a pit by his brothers? Did Moses think God was guiding when Pharaoh threw him out of Egypt? Did Hannah think God was guiding when she was childless? Did Elisha think God was leading when Jezebel lifted her tongue against him? Did Daniel and his friends think God was guiding when three of them were thrown into a fiery furnace and Daniel himself into a den of lions? Did Jonah think God was leading when he arrived in the great fish's stomach? They certainly wondered, but God was leading them all the time; just like He is leading you. I put it this way once in a little poem.

Just as he was having his toughest day,
And Goliath was coming with a lot to say,
And Israel was silent, come what may,
God was working it out for good!

Just as they thought it would never come,
And three walls surrounded Babylon,
And the people of God were sick for home,
God was working it out for good!

Just when the times were dark and dread,
And the Assyrian hosts by a fiend were led,
The angel moved and the foe lay dead,
God was working it out for good!

Just when they thought their case was lost,
They heard a knock and said, "It's a ghost",
But Peter arrived when they needed him most,
God was working it out for good!

Just stop today and bow your knee,
Though you're ready to scream and ready to flee,
Lift your heart to Him and say with me,
God is working it out for good!

Why should you worry when you have such a guide? You shouldn't. I
think of the famous singer and teenage idol, Michael Jackson, with a
ranch of 125,000 acres and millions of dollars in the bank. "What are you
sure of, Michael?", asked the T.V. presenter, Ophrah Winfrey. "I'm not
sure of anything", answered Michael. Tragically sad words, aren't they? A
christian could never say such a thing, for christians are sure of home.

They have believed and "are persuaded that He is able to keep that which they have committed to Him against that day". The emphasis is not just on WHAT Christians believe but upon WHOM they believe. Got it? Not "what" so much as "whom". He can be trusted to guide us and keep us until the very end of life.

It is a fact that the biggest tests in life do not come while you are young; they come when you are coming nearer the end of life. Satan doesn't tempt the older Christian with things he puts across the path of the younger Christian. Why? Because the older Christian knows such seemingly attractive pathways are only, in the end, unsatisfying cul-de-sacs. Satan comes to older Christians, now losing their friends and facing pain and suffering and loneliness and says, "Where is your God now?" Worry could swamp such people until they realise that the younger generation are looking to them to display what it is like to be a Christian in such circumstances. How much harder it is to face pains and aches and loneliness and difficulties without worry, and ultimately, to face, if the Lord be not come, death itself. But it can be done with such a Guide as ours.

Let me close this section with a story from my own local church that succinctly describes how worry can be overcome, even when facing death. An elder in my local church, a Godly man called Mr. Ross Pinkerton was for quite a few years a lamplighter in the Stranmillis area of Belfast. He set out at dusk each night to light the dozens of gas lamps in his district and he told me of how, as a lamplighter, he made so many friends on his route. Children would talk to him, adults would even come out of their houses and tell him their troubles. An hour before dawn, each morning, Mr. Pinkerton would set off again to put all the gas lights out.

When describing this work to me, once, he slipped in a little gem of spiritual truth. He told me that a lamplighter was once asked if he did not get awfully frightened in the dark as he set out to put out the lights. "No", he replied smiling, "When one light goes out, I keep my eye on the next one and by the time the last one is out, it is morning!"

So christians have the promise of Scripture that they will, all their days, walk in the light, no matter how dark their circumstances. God's lights of guidance are always ahead. Even when facing death, it is but the valley of the shadow and there cannot be a shadow without a light. There is even a light in the valley of death! Then it will be the dawn of eternal day. If the Lord is your light and your salvation, of whom shall you be afraid? No-one. With such a Guide, you need not even worry. Never, ever.

REFERENCES

1. E. F. Schumacher, "A Guide for the Perplexed".
    (Jonathan Cape, 1977).
2. "Matthew", William Hendriksen. New Testament Commentary.
    Banner of Truth Trust.
3. "Glory", The Biography of Billy Bray by F. W. Bourne.
    Ambassador Productions.

Backsliding

ITS CAUSES AND CURE

Her face glowed with enthusiasm. She had recently become a Christian and her lifestyle had been transformed, her attitudes changed, her destiny re-directed. She was a perfect example of a "first-love Christian". It was infectious.

As I talked with that young Christian, a mother who had found Christ in her adult life, I thought of those who start out with great enthusiasm to live for Christ but who gradually backslide in their Christian lives. They get into a state where they are not utterly indifferent but they are not fully committed, either. Like the Laodiceans, they are neither cold nor hot; they are lukewarm, tepid. They are evangelical but not evangelistic. There is no emotion, no enthusiasm no urgency, no passion or compassion in their faith. They are "faultily faultless, icily regular, splendidly null".

How do Christians get into such a state? How do they get out of it? That is what this section is all about; it is a causes-and-cure study. May God use it to show many a backslider the way home.

I. WARNING SIGNS

I well remember Space Mountain. Spending a day at Florida's Disney World had been absolutely fascinating until I noticed Space Mountain before me. I was convinced in my naivety that Space Mountain was all about the exploration of space. As I queued to enter the complex I kept coming across these signs which said, "If you are of a nervous disposition do no enter", "If you are susceptible to heart attacks do not enter", "If you have back problems do not enter", and, I thought that the signs must be for older people and carried on regardless. No experience that I can recall equals the shock I got when within minutes I rocketed into the darkness at around 70 miles per hour on one of the fastest roller coasters in the world. Believe me when I tell you that I get sick on roundabouts! I thought I was going to die! I smile a lot about it now, but it was no smiling matter at the time.

Disney World, though, is fantasy world, isn't it? Life is real. When God puts up warning signs along life's journeys it pays to heed them. We must not say, "That's for older people", or "That's for younger people". It is to our spiritual advantage to stop and say, "That's for me!". Let's check out some of the warning signs God puts up in the Scriptures. It will save a lot of backsliding and subsequent heartache if we obey them. Let me list a few.

BEWARE OF ALCOHOL

The story of Noah does not end, unfortunately, with a very pleasant record. When the man who found grace in the eyes of the Lord settled down after the trauma of the flood, he planted a vineyard. One day he got drunk and was found by his sons lying naked in his tent. The whole sorry episode had far-reaching repercussions for him and his family.

The Bible shows that alcohol is deceitful and "he who is deceived thereby is not wise". Twenty percent of males and ten percent of females in the adult population are seriously involved with alcohol. Alcohol disease is said to be the third public health problem after cancer and cardiovascular disease. The mortality of dependent and problem drinkers is three to four times that of the general population, and life expectancy is reduced by about fifteen years. Each year between eight and fourteen million working days are lost through alcohol abuse. Eight hundred million pounds are lost to industry and sickness absence due to alcohol. The Brewing Industry spends four billion pounds in advertising and three hundred thousand in research into the effects of alcohol. Advertising is directed towards young people. In a sample of sixteen to twenty-four year olds on Saturday night drinking ten percent had drunk more than seventeen units of alcohol (example, eight and a half pints of beer) and forty percent of twenty to twenty-four year old males were regularly over the legal limit. In about eighty percent of all serious road accidents, alcohol is implicated. In ninety percent of suicide attempts alcohol is involved. It causes depression to worsen, leads to impaired thinking processes, and produces impetuous actions.

My friend, Dr. Adam Hanna, writing on the subject of 'The Christian and Alcohol' recently quoted a medical expert involved in the prevention of alcohol abuse. The expert said, "Primary prevention is the activity that stops the non-hazardous drinker becoming a hazardous one, and health education is directed to this end, but there seem to be powerful, if ill-defined forces pushing many across that threshold". Dr. Hanna points out that in small or large doses the effect of alcohol on the body (the brain) is always depressant, inhibitory, i.e. negative.

Paradoxically the effect of small doses appears to be to relax, to reduce sense of stress, to give feeling of pleasure or well-being, but alcohol does that by actually depressing the normal inhibitory systems in the higher centres of the brain. For example, "social drinks" at a lunch or party are supposed to lower people's inhibitions and allow them to mix more freely, to give them a feeling of excitement or pleasure, and to reduce the normal stress of meeting strangers - but they do this by "cheating" and exerting a depressant action on protective natural inhibitions rather than giving an added excitatory action.

In any event this effect is short lived and often it takes more and more to produce the same effect. Along with this feeling of relaxation or pleasure, alcohol in small doses does several other things.

It produces a loss of general efficiency, reduces one's critical abilities, slows one reflexes, and allows one's more basic instincts to emerge. It is easy therefore to respect deeply the person (many of them non-Christians) who in the light of this picture remain life-long teetotallers. They have wisdom on their side, however else they may be regarded. The word of Scripture is a warning to us all; "Do not be drunk with wine, in which is dissipation; but be filled with the Spirit".

BEWARE OF LYING

The story of Abraham gives a very clear warning. He arrived in Canaan and found himself in a famine situation, panicked, fled into Egypt and lied to Pharaoh that his wife was his full sister because he was afraid they would kill him and take her. God sent a plague on Pharaoh's house as a result, Abraham's lying was discovered and he was thrown out of Egypt.

It was not until he got back to the point where he had got off track at a place called Bethel and there "called on the name of the Lord" that he experienced restoration from his backsliding. Forty years later, though, he again ignored the warning sign and lied again to subsequent harrowing trouble. Later in the Scriptures we read of Jacob, though having a Godly father, backslid very seriously. He deceived his old blind father into blessing him and in turn, many years later, his own sons deceived him with a blood-stained coat into believing that his beloved child Joseph was dead. What we sow, we reap.

BEWARE OF HASTE

Moses desperately wanted to free God's people. At forty years of age he saw an Egyptian beating a Hebrew and decided to kill him. It was a hasty action and led to forty years in a literal as well as spiritual wilderness. He should have waited for God's time. The little word "Selah" in the Psalms means "pause". Say it often.

BEWARE OF GREED

Achan was in Joshua's army when they took the city of Jericho. The army was warned by God not to loot; the silver and gold and vessels of bronze and iron were to be given into the Lord's treasury. Achan, though, was greedy, and stole gold and silver in Jericho for himself. As a result the whole of the nation of the Children of Israel were held up in their progress into the Promised Land until Achan's sin was dealt with. The warning from Achan's life shows that one backslider can do as much and more damage to the progress of God's work and God's people than the enemies of the Lord.

BEWARE OF IMMORALITY

Samson was a He-man with a She-weakness. Gifted with special strength from God, he fooled about with his gift instead of using it to God's glory. The most gifted believers are not always the best behaved, are they? The prostitute at Gaza, and the subtle Delilah in the valley of Sorek, made Samson court lust, but that which appeared to him as soft as down became, before it was finished, a flaming vulture.

Solomon too, the wisest man in all the earth became an effeminate fool and allowed women to turn his heart away from the Lord. His father, David, the man after God's own heart, found that a moment's indulgence wrecked his family and brought about the severing of his kingdom. The blame, please note, was not left at Bathsheba's door but David's. Purity, Christian, is power.

BEWARE OF POPULARITY

Saul, Israel's king, had Israel's army mustered at Gilgal. His enemy, the Philistines, were massed against him with thirty thousand chariots and six thousand horsemen and people "as the sand which is on the seashore in multitude". Saul had been commanded by the prophet Samuel to wait for the prophet's arrival to offer a sacrifice to the Lord before he went into battle. He waited five, six and even seven days and when Samuel did not show up, Saul's patience began to run out. His men began to scatter. You can almost hear them, can't you? "What an indecisive man is Saul". So, to be popular, he disobeyed the prophet and the Lord's commandment and offered up the sacrifice. It cost him his throne.

Peter, of course, in New Testament days, had the same problem; he wanted to be liked. His Lord and Saviour was bound and interrogated at the High's Priest's house and the servant girl there asked Peter if he were one of Christ's disciples. The result? Wanting to be liked and wanting to be popular Peter denied his Saviour on the spot. He was to regret it all his days. Beware of popularity.

Voltaire was once going past a crowd queueing to see one of his plays. "Look at that crowd, queueing to see your play", said a friend. "The same crowd would come to see me hung", he said. Too right.

BEWARE OF HYPOCRISY

No prophet ever thundered against hypocrisy like Isaiah. The Bible's word for hypocrisy has to do with play-acting, it has to do with being two-faced in a relationship with God. It is to be one thing when before God and another thing when before people. Hypocrisy just will not "wash" with God. He hates it and if, as a Christian, you are being hypocritical, then you are without doubt in a backslidden condition. If you doubt me, just meditate on these words of God spoken by Isaiah to the people of Israel. "To what purpose is the multitude of your sacrifices to me? I have had enough of burnt offerings ... when you come to appear before Me, who has required this from your hand, to trample My courts? Your New Moons and your appointed feasts My soul hates; they are a trouble to Me, I am weary of bearing them. When you spread out your hands, I will hide My eyes from you; even though you make many prayers I will not hear". (Isaiah 1; 11-15).

BEWARE OF FALLING IN LOVE WITH THE AGE YOU LIVE IN

At the very end of the Apostle Paul's life, when he was under house-arrest, there appears a little line in a letter which he wrote to his young friend, Timothy, which is quite haunting. "Demas", he wrote, "has forsaken me, having loved this present world, and has departed for Thessalonica". (2 Timothy 4; 10). What had happened? In plain language, Paul's fellow helper Demas (Philemon 24) had left the track of service; he had become a backslider.

We may be quite sure that it was not a sudden collapse. The crisis, when it came, was certainly a matter of a single fatal decision but, just as a marriage doesn't suddenly collapse without other events occurring first, just as a building doesn't suddenly collapse without cracks or faults appearing somewhere, so before Demas' defection came, his love for Christ had been burning low.

In Demas' soul, at one time, the thought of Christ's Kingdom had thrilled him, he had longed for the coming of Christ, but now, says the Bible, "he loved this present age". What made the difference? The most probable reason was that identification with Christ was becoming a very serious matter. Nero had burst into a mad fury and the Christians were bearing the brunt of his murderous mania. Paul, his friend, was under house-arrest and the verdict might go against him. Demas probably feared arrest and the Province of Macedonia would have been an infinitely safer place to live, especially since Thessalonica was a free city under Greek local Government. Demas preferred to win his own comfort than to win the lost. He loved this present age while Paul loved Christ's appearing. Paul looked to the future. Demas wanted more of the present. Paul finished the course; Demas left the track.

Let's be warned. He who loves this present age will soon become a widower. Let's never be tempted to retain situations and desert Christ, to avoid derision, and miss the reward of confessing the Lord. May the Lord find that we choose Him rather than our own ease and prefer to face the storm by His side to basking in the sunshine alone.

In the great Cathedral in Frieberg, Germany, the organist would allow no-one to play the massive pipe organ but himself. He guarded the superb instrument, jealously. One day a man came into the Cathedral and gently asked if he could play it. The organist was extremely reluctant to give permission but eventually relented. The stranger played the organ like it had never been played before. "Can I ask your name?", asked the Cathedral organist. "Felix Mendelssohn" was the reply. "To think", the Cathedral organist used to say, "I very nearly didn't let the Master play the organ".

Let's make sure the Master of our lives has His way. Let's heed the warning signs He has put out for us in His Word. If we do we will never regret it for we will be preserved from backsliding and be enabled to live our lives to His glory.

2. TWO BACKSLIDERS INVESTIGATED

He was a true believer. He hated wrongdoing with a holy hatred. He was a child of God and an heir of the Kingdom. It would be easy to read his case-notes and go away saying he was a no-good, but, the Bible won't let us. Yet, he became a backslider. So much so, two angels had to virtually drag him out of the city where he lived before God destroyed it. His name was Lot. How on earth did he get into such a spiritual state?

It is true that Sodom, the city where Lot lived, was a very sinful place, but, Lot did not become accustomed to what went on in it. He was a just and righteous man and, 2 Peter 2; 7-8 says he had his righteous soul tormented from day to day by seeing and hearing the lawless deeds of the unrighteous around him. Yet, despite this, Lot slipped into a tepid state of soul. What word sums it all up? The answer is given in Genesis 19; 16. It says, "He lingered". He knew the awful condition of the city where he lived, hated its practices, but, when two angels were sent from God urging him to get out, he lingered.

He believed God always kept His Word, but, he lingered. "Arise", they cried, "Take your wife and your two daughters who are here, lest you be consumed in the punishment of the city". Yet, he lingered until the angels "took hold of his hand......and brought him out and set him out- side the city".

What was it that drew Lot into such a dithering, lukewarm commitment to his Lord? The answer is that he made a wrong and selfish choice in his early life. There was strife between the herdsmen of his uncle Abraham and his own herdsmen when Lot had lived with Abraham and Abraham decided they had better split up. Abraham said, "You take left, I'll go right; you go right, then I'll go left".

What did Lot do? Without any prayer for guidance he stood up and looked out the best land and water in all the country around him and without a moment's hesitation "chose for himself all the plane of Jordan". Note those two words "for himself".

Lot well knew the name and character of the city of Sodom that lay in the rain and sunshine before him but, as J. C. Ryle commented, "Lot's cattle were already up to their stomachs in the grass around Sodom and that was heaven on earth to Lot..... The pasture was rich, the land was good. He wanted such country for his flocks and herds and before that argument all scruples and doubts, if indeed he had any, at once went down".

First he "looked" (Genesis 13; 10), then he "pitched his tent towards Sodom" (Genesis 13; 12). Then he "dwelt" in Sodom (Genesis 14; 12).

Nothing wrong with Sodom if God wants you there. Nothing wrong with "well watered plains" if God sends you there. But, better a wilderness and little money and the blessing of God and the joy of the Lord in your soul than to go to Sodom out of the will of God. Lot did no good in Sodom. Not one of his neighbours believed his witness nor cared one hoot for his opinion. His salt lost its savour; his wife turned into a pillar of salt when she disobeyed God and his two daughters escaped to do the Devil's work. We leave Lot in the pages of Genesis, a poor drunken, miserable wretch living in a cave.

So, Christian, beware of your choices. Remember when you choose a house or a flat in which to settle down, comfort, good location and reasonable rent or price isn't everything. When you choose a career it will cost you nothing if you make a lot of money and have leanness in your soul at the same time. Don't linger; ask God's guidance before you make a choice and put Him first in all that you do. If you make selfish choices you will end like Lot, saved from the fire but losing out eternally on the reward. (Read very carefully Paul's warning in 1 Corinthians 3; 12-15).

Let us now investigate a character who was the very opposite to Lot. He obeyed God meticulously in his early life. He chose wisely and prayerfully. With 300 men and the power of God he turned an army that lay like "sand by the seashore in multitude" into flight. Even before he defeated the Midianites he cut down the totem pole to a false god in his own father's back yard and instead of his father turning against him, his father became his greatest supporter. He was used by God to restore his own father from gross backsliding. His name? Gideon.

What happened to such a godly man? How did the man who was able to control the unity of his army through prayer and who was able to keep the supply line of food going when most of his fellow compatriots had fled to the hills for fear of the enemy, become a backslider? It all started with him losing his temper.

If we could leave the story of Gideon with his subduing of the Midianities, Gideon's story would have been a happy story indeed, but, the Bible record of his life goes on in all realism to tell us that the wonderful fruits of victory were flawed. It shows us that Satan is a very dirty fighter. We read that as Gideon pursued the Midianites, the men of Ephraim, part of God's people, couldn't rejoice in Gideon's victory. Why? Because they had not been "called up" and since they didn't have a part in his victory, they couldn't rejoice.

They even "gave off" to Gideon as he was pursuing the enemy during his great victory. Jealousy, of course, always hinders the work of God. "Why", said Gideon, "What have I done in comparison with you? Is not the gleaning of the grapes of Ephraim better than the vintage of Abiezer?". Gideon, in other words, took the low place; he subtly reminded the men of Ephraim of their position as the largest tribe in Israel who lived in a much richer track of country than he did. He knew that a soft answer always turns away wrath. So, he let them go, wasn't diverted by the Devil's ploy and went on pursuing the enemy.

If only Gideon had kept up such a wise attitude. But the Devil pursued him yet again and tried to "ditch him" with the men of Succoth. The men of Succoth had no fewer than seventy elders and seven princes at their head. They were part of God's people and Gideon asked them, "Please give loaves of bread to the people who follow me, for they are exhausted". But the leaders of Succoth replied that since Gideon hadn't won yet, why should they give bread to his army?

Mark it well that the men of Succoth were the Lord's people and Gideon was the Lord's appointed representative. When they refused to help Gideon, they were in reality refusing to help the Lord. Yet, it is at this very point that Gideon began to slip back. Backsliding, you see, can begin by our reaction for life is ten percent what happens to us and ninety percent how we react to it.

Why did Gideon not let them go, like he did the men of Ephraim? I do not know, but, instead of answering them quietly and going on with his work for the Lord, he promised that when he returned after victory over the enemy he would tear their flesh with the thorns of the wilderness and with briars. And he did just that. Nasty, miserable thorns that the curse produced were used by Gideon to cut his brethren down to size. He found a young man from the city, interrogated him, wrote down the seventy elders names, took the thorns of the wilderness and thrashed the elders of Succoth. Later at a place called Penuel Gideon got the same treatment as he had received at Succoth and he came back and tore down the tower of Penuel and killed the men of the city.

See what backsliding can do? Whose side was Gideon fighting on, now? Would the men of Penuel not need their defence?

Would the men of Succoth not need their elders? Temper was the undoing of Gideon at the end of a time of great blessing. He was a great man but he didn't remove the needle in his tongue. Anger is a God-given emotion but bad temper is a sin. Gideon ended up fighting the Lord's people instead of the Lord's enemies. It marred his great witness.

Let's learn lessons from the lives of Lot and Gideon for if we do it will be a cure for much backsliding and a prevention of more.

• Beware of the choices you make (Proverbs 3; 5-6).

• Make sure that your choices in life are not made from a selfish motive (Genesis 13; 11).

• Do not "linger" between commitment to God's command and commitment to your own desires (Genesis 19; 15-16).

• Make sure that you do not allow your choices to lead you to material wealth at the cost of sending leanness into your soul (Psalm 106; 15).

- Make sure you do not merely escape hell and lose out on eternal rewards in Heaven by building "wood, hay and stubble" in your life (I Corinthians 3; 12-15).

- Learn to ignore petty disagreements (Proverbs 19; 11).

- Refrain from close association with anger-prone people (Proverbs 22; 24-25).

- Keep a close check on your tongue (Proverbs 15; 1).

- Control your anger or it will control you (Proverbs 25; 28).

3. A LETTER TO BACKSLIDERS

How would you feel if, at your local church, you received a letter directly from the Lord? It would make an interesting Sunday morning if it was read out, publicly, detailing the Lord's view of what He thought about the spiritual condition of your local church and all its members.

Other opinions of your local church could be argued with but the Lord's opinion is different.

He has full executive power and authority over His church and, being the perfect One, His summary of how you stood would allow no arguments. This Judge's opinion is final.

Such was the situation when the Apostle John received a revelation of the Lord's Word to the seven churches recorded in the book of the Revelation. The letters were actually written to seven churches existing at the time in Asia but they carry an even wider message because they give a picture of seven conditions of Christians and their church life to be found continuously in the history of the Church of Christ.

Their message is very relevant to our subject of backsliding for they give a clear "causes-and-cure" analysis of certain spiritual conditions.

The letters contain good things Christ found in His churches but they also contain Christ's complaints and His superb counsel as to how His people could reverse their condition.

No Christian could study them but to his or her advantage. Let's have a look at a few of these letters.

THE EPHESUS LETTER

The Church in the wealthy, cultured but corrupt city of Ephesus had been planted by Paul, greatly aided by his friends Aquila and Priscilla, the tentmakers. Had you visited it you would have reckoned it to be the most outstanding Christian church you ever saw in your life. True church order was in place, the ministry was first rate, the administration was fine. The Lord had several good things to say about the Ephesian church.

"I know your works", said the Lord. Here was no passive group of Christians; they were very active for their Master. "I know your tribulation". These Christians were not afraid of the cost of living for Christ.

"I know your patience". They were no quitters, these Ephesian Christians. On and on they went, week in and week out, year in and year out. "I know you cannot bear those that are evil", is Christ's opinion of the way they guarded their fellowship from impure men and women. "I know you have tested those who say they are apostles and are not and have found them to be liars", comments the Lord. No false doctrine found its way into the church at Ephesus.

"And you have persevered and have patience and have laboured for my Name's sake and have not become weary". Persecution didn't swamp the courage of the saints at Ephesus. They were true to their Lord.

What, then, could possibly be wrong with such a church? How could you find a backslider in the whole place? Truth was, they were all backsliders! "Now", says the Lord of the churches, "I have this against you that you have left your first love". That's it! A single sentence, but, devastating in its analysis. The church was busy, orthodox, sound, faithful but lacking in emotion and enthusiasm. You know how it is. A fellow falls in love and first love defies analysis. Ask him why he loves and he can't tell you. His love is pure, unselfish, ardent, humble. It isn't forced, it isn't a duty, it is full of tenderness. Dr. G. Campbell Morgan put it perfectly when he said the Lord no longer heard "the song at the unusual hour" from the Ephesian Christians. They were "faultily faultless, icily regular, splendidly null".

And the cure? "Repent therefore from where you have fallen; repent and do the first works, or else I will come to you quickly and remove your lampstand from its place - unless you repent". The Lord tells them to turn back in heart and purpose to their first attitude to Him. He tells them to believe in Him in the way they used to.

Else? Else despite all their ice-cold purity and orthodoxy, their church will be removed. The message to the backsliders of Ephesus or the backsliders of this present century could not be clearer. Selah.

THE PERGAMOS LETTER

We would probably call Pergamos a "New Age" city in our day.

Aesculapius, the god of medicine was worshipped there and the special aspect of this worship was the study of the secret springs of life. Like all Nature worship, it was sincere but brought with it much corruption. The church at Pergamos was faithful to the Lord, even to the death, for one of its members, Antipas, was martyred for Christ, there. But they had a problem. Some of their number believed "the doctrine of Balaam" which simply stated held that since you were the Lord's you needn't worry too much about how you behaved.

Many backsliders are like that. Because they believe that once a person is saved, they are always saved (which, incidentally, I also believe), they also think that a believer's behaviour will make no difference to their Heaven.

Nothing could be further from the truth. A study of the story of the prodigal son and the immediate parable of the shrewd manager which follows it (Luke chps. 15 and 16) will show very clearly that the Christian will lose out on eternal reward by ungodly behaviour after their conversion.

Not only will people who "hold the doctrine of Balaam" lose out, eternally, their doctrine is a pernicious, dangerous poison in the body of the local church. The Lord counsels the Christians at Pergamos to deal with these people by showing both them and their doctrine no toleration. He warns them to discipline these people or else He will discipline them Himself.

There is, in the letter to Pergamos, a beautiful promise given to the person who overcomes. To such an overcomer the Lord says He will give a "white stone, and on the stone a new name written which no one knows except him who receives it". What does this mean? A white stone was given to a person who, after a trial, was justly acquitted. It was also given to one who returned victorious from battle. It was the reward of victory. The white stone was given to a person who was made a free man of the city. But, there is an even greater meaning.

There was the white stone known as the tessara hospitalis. Two men, friends, about to part, would divide a white stone in two, each carrying with him half, upon which was inscribed the name of the friend. It may be they would never meet again, but that stone in each case would be bequeathed to a son, and sometimes generations after, a man would meet another, and they would find that they possessed the complementary halves of one white stone, and their friendship would be at once created upon the basis of the friendship made long ago.

So it is that for the overcomer there is the white stone of acquittal, the white stone of victory, and the white stone of citizenship, which marks the freedom of the city of God. Best of all, though, is the white stone of unending friendship, my name written on His half, His Name written on mine.

The central message of the Pergamos letter to the backslider of today is an extremely solemn one. It is that the test of doctrine is purity of conduct and character. What we believe is extremely important but how we behave is equally so.

THE SARDIS LETTER

The Lord's complaint about the Christians at Sardis was startling, to say the least. "I know your works", He said, "That you have a name that your are alive, but you are dead. Be watchful and strengthen the things that remain, that are ready to die, for I have not found your works perfect before God". It was a devastating appraisal of a very frightening spiritual condition. What was it? It was outward observance of spiritual things and inward spiritual deadness. Nothing they did satisfied God. It looked great on paper, it sounded wonderful in the committee room, but death reigned. The church at Sardis had a wonderful reputation amongst others but before God it was dead.

"Establish the things that remain", counsels the Lord. If the church at Sardis was dead, what on earth could have remained? The unfulfilled things. They met to break bread and drink wine in remembrance of Christ's death but now they were called on to truly do that.

They met to pray but now they were called on to truly pray. They had gifts, now they were to exercise those gifts to the full to God's glory. No church can exist on mere formal gatherings or on mere organisational ability, it needs to respond to the leadership of the Spirit of God which is its vital force. What we need here in the western world is not yet another Christian denomination but a mighty breath of God through us as we are, today.

THE LETTER TO THE LAODICEANS

If ever there was a word from the Lord to backsliders it is found in His letter to the Laodiceans. "I know your works, that you are neither cold nor hot. I could wish that you were cold or hot. So then, because you are lukewarm, and neither cold nor hot, I will spew you out of my mouth. Because you say, 'I am rich, have become wealthy, and have need of nothing' - and do not know that you are wretched, miserable, poor, blind, and naked - I counsel you to buy from me gold refined in the fire, that you may be rich; in white garments, that you may be clothed, that the shame of your nakedness may not be revealed; and anoint your eyes with eye salve, that you may see. As many as I love, I rebuke and chasten. Therefore be zealous and repent.

Behold I stand at the door and knock. If anyone hears My voice and opens the door, I will come in to him and dine with him, and he with Me."

I want to use the teaching in this letter to bring our study to its conclusion. The letter is both exquisitely sad and, yet, exquisitely beautiful. Here is a church which is neither hot nor cold. It thought it was rich and had need of nothing and, yet, says the Lord, "You are wretched, miserable, poor, blind and naked".

Note its spiritual condition. It wasn't frozen, nor was it boiling. It was lukewarm, tepid. The Lord said to them, "I could wish you were cold or hot", but He detests their lukewarmness. As someone once put it, "They were evangelical but not evangelistic". Is there anything, in all the world, which is so repugnant to the Lord as a tepid church? The Lord so detested their lukewarmness - He said He would spew them out of His mouth.

He did not mean He was going to break His eternal relationship with them but it did mean He was about to take the church at Laodicea away from its place of witness. He was about to put out the light of its witness-bearing. He had not done it yet, but He was about to.

Could it be that you are just like the Laodiceans? He said that they were "wretched", that is, carrying a burden where outwardly they appear to be doing very well and in need of nothing. Actually their wealth was hindering them. Is that you? He said they were "miserable", that is, pitiable. He pitied them. Is that you? He said they were "poor", that is, so poor all they had was money! Is that you? He said they were "blind", that is, they could see nothing clearly! Is that you? He said they were "naked", that is, outwardly wearing gold and beautiful clothes but gold that was tarnished and clothes that were moth-eaten in the light of a robe of true service for Christ. Is that you?

What was the cure the Lord offered? "I counsel you", He said, "to buy from Me gold refined in the fire, that you may be rich". The Lord has what the Laodiceans and any other backslider lacks. He has true wealth. If any backslider will get down on their knees before the Lord and admit their spiritual condition, then the Lord will reward them with things that He considers to be wealth, things that have eternal consequences, gold that never tarnishes. He pleads that you buy that kind of gold from Him and be truly rich. Will you?

He then promises "white garments that you may be clothed". Sin can be forgiven, the backslider can be restored, and we need, as Paul put it, no longer make provision for the flesh but we need to "put on the Lord Jesus". What a covering for our spiritual nakedness!

Finally He says, "Anoint your eyes with eye salve, that you may see". No chemist's potion ever had a more powerful effect than the Lord's eye salve on a backslider's eyes. He can make you see things as you never saw them before. He can give you insight the world knows nothing of. Don't stumble on in a half-baked, lukewarm, tepid, neither hot-nor-cold Christian life. Buy the Lord's gold, put on His garments, let Him, this very moment place His eye salve on your tired and weary eyes. He says, "Behold I stand at the door and knock. If anyone hears My voice and opens the door, I will come in to him and dine with him and he with Me". These beautiful words were first spoken to a backsliding church. They are now spoken to backsliders everywhere. Will you open up the door and let Him in? The choice is yours.

Suffering

A BIBLICAL PERSPECTIVE ON
LIFE'S GREATEST PUZZLE

No greater challenge arises to faith than when, suddenly, trauma and heartache surge into a person's life. Suffering can come in many forms; it can come in the form of a broken love affair, an unhappy marriage, a business collapse or sudden unemployment. Perhaps its most traumatic form is when a child or teenager dies in a family and a parent lifts a weary head and asks that searing, burning question; "How could a loving God let this happen?"

Doubt, depression and loneliness often follow suffering and the sometimes inexplicable silence of God in it all can be most unsettling. People begin to feel that either God is not good or not Almighty, or begin to wonder if He is there at all. In our world of starving millions, terrorist outrages, and wars by the hundred, suffering people right across the earth cry for some meaning to the bizarre things happening all around them.

Is there a Biblical perspective on life's greatest puzzle?

Is there a clear-cut answer to suffering?

Let's investigate.

1. THE TOUR OF ALL TOURS

It is important to remember, right at the beginning of our investigation, that pain is essential to normal life on this planet. The pain network in our bodies has some remarkable features. For example: Without pain warnings, most sports would be too risky. Without pain, art and culture would be very limited. Without pain, our lives would be in mortal danger.

Those rare people who feel no pain have no warning of a ruptured appendics, heart attack or brain tumour. Without pain, musicians would have real problems. A guitarist, for example, must be able to feel exactly where his finger lands on the string and how hard it presses. Musicians rely on the body's sensitivity to pain and pressure. Without pain, there would be no sex, for sexual pleasure is mostly carried by pain cells. Pain is not something God thought up at the last moment to make our lives miserable. The millions of pain sensors in our bodies show God's intricate care for us. [1]

Human suffering, though, involves more than pain. The Bible doesn't shrink from this fact, it steams right into it with the story of a man called Job. A whole book in the Bible is given to his story, a book of forty-two chapters. It is probably the oldest book in the world and the oldest statement of the never ending problem of human suffering.

At the outset, Job is placed before us as the model of a perfect man, the very paragon of his age. Rich and prosperous, he has seven sons and three daughters and is enjoying a very happy family life. He has a vast estate and immense possessions and seems to fit the popular equation that personal goodness plus happy outward conditions equals the normal result of the righteous rule of God.

Suddenly, in one single day, Job, through a series of disasters and catastrophies, is deprived of his flocks and herds, his faithful servants and his loving children. As if such losses were not enough for any human to bear, his health breaks down and a horrible skin disease covers his entire body. The sore, angry swellings cause Job long and restless nights and as he is no longer able to work, he goes and sits down "Among the ashes" (Job 2;8). In all villages and cities of the east, the local rubbish dump was burned once a month and the ashes remained. If the city or village had been inhabited for a century, the rubbish dump known as the mezbele, reached quite a height. It gradually turned into a firm round mound of earth and served the inhabitants of the district as a watch tower and on close oppressive evenings as a place of assembly because there is a current of air on the height. There the children would play all day long and there the forsaken lay, by day asking alms of the passersby and at night hiding among the ashes which the sun had warmed.

Our investigation of human suffering leads us, then, to this poor man, bereaved, humiliated and in pain, sitting in a rubbish dump. His skin is festering, his nerves are on fire. Does the Bible present him sitting with a "stiff upper lip", unmoved by it all? Certainly not. He curses the very day he was born. (See Job 3; 1). Few people in history have described as graphically as Job how very wretched human existence can be. He declares that it would have been better never to have existed at all. He even curses the night of his conception and says "May it not be included among the days of the year". (Job 3; 6). He longs for death (Job 3; 11-19) and it seems the sole good left to him. Let no-one ever say that the Bible isn't realistic. Like millions of human beings after him, Job found life intolerable and death desirable, even a relief. Millions can identify with Job's words when he said; "Oh that my grief were fully weighed, and my calamity laid out in the balances, for then it would be heavier than the sand on the sea .... for the arrows of the Almighty are within me; my spirit drinks in their poison" (Job 6; 2-4). Job couldn't relax, he couldn't settle or rest, he was highly agitated and accused God of firing arrows at him.

In all of this the most surprising element is that God does not berate Job. God lets him pour out his grief and frustration and sorrow. He doesn't even interrupt him. Job's friends, though, have plenty to say and their interruptions are frequent.

They have a doctrine that says that God is good to the good and bad to the bad, and they rub it in to poor Job. They claim that Job must have sinned, else he wouldn't be suffering. "All his days the wicked man suffers torment", says Eliphaz (Job 15: 20). "The lamp of the wicked is snuffed out", adds Bildad (Job 18: 5) and to cap it all, Zophar says "The mirth of the wicked is brief" (Job 20:5). "Is not your wickedness great", they conclude, "Are not your sins endless?". (Job 22:5).

The interesting thing is that God does not accept the spiritual diagnosis of Job's three friends. He condemns what they have said as folly. (Job 42; 7-8). From this we learn in our investigation of human suffering, that God does not always use pain or suffering as a punishment. That He has done is shown in the history of the children of Israel but in every case, the punishment that they got follows repeated warnings against the behaviour that merits the punishment. Even the AIDS epidemic of our day is not without warning in Scripture. (Romans 1: 26-27). The prophets in Israel's day consistently warned of the dire consequences of Israel's behaviour.

Our friend Job, though, was not suffering as a result of wrongdoing any more than the blind man that Jesus spoke of in John 9; 1-5.

Why then did Job suffer? Job never found out in this life, yet, millions of us who read the book of Job can now see that his suffering was the testing ground of a proposition put by Satan to God which, simply summed-up, asks, "Is a person capable of loving God even though there is no evident proof of God's love in their life and even though they don't, in this life, gain by loving God, but lose?". In other words, can God inspire affection in human beings, even though He does not appear to be affectionate? Until Christ came, the fact is that no individual soul ever made such a battle ground between God's power and the Devil's power as Job's soul did.

Job couldn't hide his despair with himself and with what God was allowing to happen to him, but, Job stuck to the point day and night that God is righteous and has a purpose, although everything in his actual experience seemed to prove the very opposite. In the midst of it all, Job's incredible leap of faith has since sent waves of courage to all suffering souls. The Bible tells us that his pain was so great that he "Took his flesh in his teeth", i.e. Job was in such misery he even bit his own flesh to ease the pain (Job 13; 14). Superbly, in the midst of his great personal suffering, Job suddenly makes one of the greatest statements of faith in all history; "Though He slay me, yet will I trust Him", he says (Job 13; 15).

What was God's answer to all that Job suffered? Did God say that He had power but not enough power to solve human suffering? Did He say that the mess this world was in was too much for Him? No, he took Job for a tour of tours and showed Him his creative genius. Job learned, in spite of his personal suffering, to trust God again because he was overwhelmed by the display of God's power in creation. Of course, the critics have poured scorn on God's response to Job's sufferings. George Bernard Shaw in "The Adventures of the Black Girl in Her Search for God" has her call the Lord's speech "A sneer". It is far from a sneer. God invites Job to meet him like a man (Job 38; 3) and never hints that it is not for him to question the ways of the Almighty. "The aim", one writer comments, "is not to crush Job. On the contrary, the mere fact that God converses with him gives him a dignity above all the birds and beasts, assuring him that it is a splendid thing to be a man. To look at any bird or flower is a revelation of God in His constant care for His world. Here is the proof that a person can love God for simply being God, not for reward. Here the lack of a formal answer to a moral question, indeed the narrowing of the spotlight of the book to one individual, is positively instructive."

What a tour God gives Job! In Chapter 38 of Job we read of God discussing the origin of the sea (v. 8-11), here is the miracle of the daily appearance of the day (v. 12-15), here is the vast subterranean region (v. 16-18). Here are the treasures of the snow (verse 22-23) or the rainstorm (v. 24-27). God shows Job the dew and ice and hoar frost and the great constellations of Pleiades and Orion (verse 28-33). God even teaches Job that no person can fully understand the movements of clouds (v. 34-38).

God then moves to things that are closer to Job. Man has been placed in charge of the world and yet no-one can "Hunt the prey for the lion or satisfy the appetite for the young lions". Yet, God is the primary cause for doing that very thing. Even the ravens are fed by Him (v. 39-41).

The tour continues as God displays to Job his intricate knowledge of the Ibex goat and his supervision of the breeding of their flocks. Instinct in animals is God's creation (39;1-4). The wild ass is wild because God made him wild (39; 1,5,16). The extinct Aurochs, (extinct since 1627) the most powerful of all hoofed beasts is discussed (39; 9-12) and even the ridiculousness of the ostrich is discussed in humorous detail (39; 13-18). The horse was never more perfectly described (39; 19-25) and the hawk and the eagle are pin-pointed (39;26-30).

To all of this and more, on the tour, Job's response is to worship God and trust Him again.

Job never gets to what really lies behind all his suffering, but he sees God in such a way that he doesn't need to. He trusts the God of creation and even though his suffering, bereavement and pain continue, he moves from asserting and defending himself to surrendering to God. The test Satan set would only work if Job did not know what the test was for. That is why it worked because Job never discovered what his suffering was about during his lifetime. Even though God's purpose in the details of Job's suffering life were not clear to Job, that did not stop him from trusting God and from crying out in the midst of his pain, "For I know that my Redeemer lives and He shall stand at last on the earth; and after my skin is destroyed, this I know, that in my flesh I shall see God, whom I shall see for myself, and my eyes shall behold, and not another". (Job 19; 25-27). What have we learned, then, from the story of Job about suffering?

We have learned:-

1.   Personal suffering is not necessarily a result of personal sin.

2. Suffering can be the testing ground of the fact that a person can have affection for God even though God does not appear to be affectionate.

3. Suffering is not the proof that God is not all powerful.

4. Suffering raises great dilemmas and questions and it is certainly not a sin to ask questions to God when overwhelmed with difficult circumstances. God can and eventually will answer all our questions.

5. Suffering may surround us but we can learn to trust God again through an insight into His creative genius.

6. Suffering may give no clue to what God is up to in our personal circumstances but that is no reason for refusing to worship Him. We must allow God to know some things we don't.

Recently, while visiting Oxford University for the preaching of God's Word, I took a tour of the city on an open topped bus. My mind went back to that famous day in 1929 when the atheistic C. S. Lewis was going up Headington Hill in Oxford on the top of a bus when he became aware that he was holding God "At bay". He writes, "Amiable agnostics will talk cheerfully about 'Man's search for God'. To me, as I then was, they might as well have talked about the mouse's search for the cat!". Later that evening the result of the long conviction of his mind and heart by the Holy Spirit came to a head and Lewis asks us to picture him alone in his room at Magdalen College. "Night after night, feeling, whenever my mind lifted even for a second from my work, the steady, unrelenting approach of Him whom I so earnestly desired not to meet. That which I greatly feared had at last come upon me. In the Trinity Term of 1929, I gave in, and admitted that God was God, and knelt and prayed: perhaps that night the most dejected and reluctant convert in all England. I did not then see what is now the most shining and obvious thing; the Divine humility which will accept a convert even on such terms.

The Prodigal Son at least walked home on his own feet. But who can duly adore that Love which will open the high gates to a prodigal who is brought in kicking, struggling, resentful, and darting his eyes in every direction for a chance of escape?

The words "compelle intrare", compel them to come in, have been so abused by wicked men that we shudder at them; but properly understood, they plumb the depths of the Divine mercy. The hardness of God is kinder than the softness of men, and His compulsion is our liberation."[2]

If C. S. Lewis was a reluctant convert, he became an outstanding believer. So it was that though Job questioned and accused, raged and rampaged about the meaning of life and the horror of suffering, he certainly became one of the most outstanding believers in history. With Oswald Chambers I want to say, "Next to Jesus, Job must surely be the greatest believer in the whole Bible". Let's move on, then, to investigate suffering in the life of the Lord Jesus.

2. GOD IN PAIN

When Stephen Speilberg produced his Box Office hit film E.T., millions were moved to weep when they saw it. Speilberg said the film was his "Cry to the stars for a friend". As most science fiction stories make all alien characters a threat to our existence, Speilberg decided to create a character who would come to love us. In the film the character Extra Terrestrial was found by an American boy in the backyard of his own home.

When we think of millions of people weeping at a Holywood fantasy, the tragedy is that the story of the Gospel, which is in every respect true, seems to move so few. God, incarnate, was literally found in the back yard of an inn by some shepherds during the reign of Caesar Augustus at the height of the Roman Empire. Here was no alien creature come to love us, here was God of very God wrapped in swaddling clothes and lying in a manger. "There was no beauty that we should desire Him", said the prophet Isaiah of the event, long before it happened. In other words, Christ had no halo of light around His head, He smiled and cried and had to be fed and was dependent on His mother and had to learn to talk like any other child.

The incarnation of God has very wonderful lessons to teach us about the whole question of human suffering. God does not address us from the clouds, or from a pulpit, or through a tract on the street, but to reach us He becomes one of us and to do that involved suffering like us.

Did He suffer? No-one ever suffered like He did. He was called a Man of Sorrows. In Hebrew the word for "sorrows" is "kaab" meaning "to be in pain". So, literally, Christ was a "Man of Pains".

From the very beginning of His earthly life to His death, He was surrounded by pain of all kinds, both external and internal, both physical and psychological. The legitimacy of His birth was doubted. His family, when He began His earthly ministry, thought He was out of His mind. When His own home town crowd heard about His actions they said, "He has lost His senses". The Scribes concluded that He was in league with the Devil and said so. He was betrayed by one of His closest friends, faced false charges, was tried by a prejudiced jury and convicted by a cowardly judge. He was tortured. He was then taken out and crucified, forsaken by His disciples, His nation and finally by God the Father. He was indeed a Man of Sorrows.

"Where do broken hearts go?", Whitney Houston used to sing. We answer that they had best go to Gethsemane and Calvary for they will find a sympathy there which is not to be found anywhere else. It is a very profound experience for all suffering people to meditate upon the pain that Christ suffered in His last hours.

It is sacred ground and as we now approach it, we shall have to tread softly as we look on our suffering Lord, the "Lifter-up of our heads".

We come first across the Cedron valley and begin to climb the Mount of Olives and turn off into an olive orchard known as Gethsemane. Christ had often met there with His disciples but this time something happens which the world has never seen, before or since. It cries out for an explanation and pulls back the curtain on what the cross meant to the Saviour. We are told that He went forward alone by Himself to pray and was "Overwhelmed with sorrow to the point of death". Frightening terms are employed by the Gospels to describe Christ's mental anguish. Loathing, aversion, appalled reluctance, alarmed dismay, and consternation are part of the original language used to describe His suffering at this point.

The Saviour's reluctance to drink the bitter cup before Him was not because He was reluctant to face death or because He was afraid His friends would desert Him. It was not even fear of His enemies that overwhelmed Him. Charles II for example faced execution fearlessly. Was England's King braver than the Son of God? No. The fact remains that in that cup the Saviour had to drink was the divine punishment Christ had to bear when He was to "Bear our sins in His own body on the tree". So great was His anguish that His sweat was like drops of blood falling to the ground. Truly, if the anticipation of the cross was so tormenting, what must the real thing have been like?

Soon He was betrayed and roughly treated like a common criminal and taken away by soldiers from Gethsemane. He was spitten upon, beaten and bound. A crown of thorns was placed on His sacred head and He was mocked. They drove spikes into His hands and feet and when He was hung on the cross, darkness was all over the land from twelve noon to three p.m. It was an outward symbol of the spiritual darkness which enveloped Him. He came out of that darkness crying "My God, My God, why have You forsaken Me?" Sadly, Lloyd Webber and Rice in their rock opera "Jesus Christ Superstar" take this statement to signify that Christ was doubting His mission and make the cross out to be a good plan gone all wrong. Millions of people have been influenced by this thinking and believe it to be the truth. It was no such thing. Christ's death was no mistake but rather a Divine atonement for our sins. He came to die and

His orphan cry on the cross was a quotation from Psalm 22, verse 1; "My God, my God, why have You forsaken Me?". The very same Psalm answers the question by giving the reason for the Father's abandonment of the Son on the cross. It states, "You are Holy" (Psalm 22; 3). The Father forsook His Son in those dreadfully dark hours because of His holiness. "For He made Him who knew no sin to be sin for us, that we might become the righteousness of God in Him" (2 Corinthians 5; 21).

He was utterly alone and bore the penalty we deserved and when it was through He gave the most challenging cry in all the Scriptures; "Teletestai", which in the perfect tense means "it has been and will for ever remain finished". No work was ever more perfect.

Are you suffering? Are you beside yourself with shame or despair? Are you weary? Stand by the cross with the blind and personally suffering George Matheson and say,

"O cross that liftest up my head, I dare not ask to fly from Thee, I lay in dust life's glory dead, And from the ground there blossoms red, Life that shall endless be". There is no telling whose eye might fall on this little book and, burdened one, I call you to meditate for a moment on the following priceless texts. They come from One who knows what you are going through more than anyone ever can.

"Come to me, all you labour and are heavy laden, and I will give you rest. Take my yoke upon you and learn from Me, for I am gently and lowly in heart, and you will find rest for your souls. For My yoke is easy and my burden is light". (Matthew 11;28-29).

"There is therefore now no condemnation to those who are in Christ Jesus, who do not walk according to the flesh, but according to the Spirit. For the law of the Spirit of life in Christ Jesus has made me free from the law of sin and death". (Romans 8; 1-2).

"Who shall bring a charge against God's elect? It is God who justifies. Who is He who condemns? It is Christ who died, and furthermore is also risen, who is even at the right hand of God, who also makes intercession for us. Who shall separate us from the love Christ? Shall tribulation, or distress, or persecution, or famine, or nakedness, or peril, or sword? .... For I am persuaded that neither death nor life, nor angels nor principalities nor powers, nor things present nor things to come, nor height nor depth, nor any other created thing, shall be able to separate us from the love of God which is in Christ Jesus our Lord". (Romans 8; 33-35, 38-39).

As we think of the cross, it is very important, then, that we ask what the relationship is between Christ's pain and ours. Here are six very helpful links:

1. The cross of Christ is a stimulus to patient endurance. (Hebrews 12; 1-3).

2. The cross of Christ is the path to mature holiness. (Hebrews 5; 8-9), i.e. Christ's sufferings were the testing ground in which His obedience became full grown or mature.

3. The cross of Christ is the symbol of suffering service. (John 12; 23-26: Ephesians 3; 1-13: Colossians 1; 24: 2 Timothy 2; 8-10).

4. The cross of Christ is the hope of final glory. i.e. The hope of glory makes suffering bearable. (Romans 8; 28).

5. The cross of Christ is the ground of reasonable faith. (Romans 8; 32).

6. The cross of Christ is the proof of God's solitary love. (John 3; 16). [3]

It is true that suffering is part of life, and suffering is an alien intrusion into God's good world and will have no place or part in the New Heaven and the New Earth. It is also true that we can bring suffering on ourselves. When we neglect or abuse our bodies, we will suffer the consequences. Cirrhosis of the liver can come through the drinking of alcohol. A reckless driver may break his neck. We have no right to hold it against God if we suffer a consequence of our foolish choices. Yet, sin apart, God has joined us in our suffering and the cross of Christ certainly calls us to trust Christ as Saviour and pin our hope in a God who is constantly working out a purpose. I shall never forget approaching a friend of mine, badly injured in his eye by a terrorist bomb, to seek to comfort him. He turned to me gently and said; "If God can bring order out of the chaos of the cross, He can bring order out of the chaos of my face". Despite all the problems surrounding the question of suffering, one thing is clear; Philip Yancey has put it this way: "Consistently the Bible directs the issue away from a question of cause to a question of response". "Is God fair?" we ask in the midst of our pain. "I am in control, no matter how it looks" is God's only answer. And, then, He has a question for us, one question; "Do you trust Me?". When I see the cross, I say, yes. Do you?

3. SUFFERING CAN BE PRODUCTIVE

In the former chapter we have seen that the Lord Jesus demonstrated that blessing comes through suffering and I now want to show from Scripture and from life the irreputable fact that there are a cloud of witnesses that prove this principle to be true. I want to show that it is as important "what" we get out of suffering as "that" we get out of it. Scripture shows that all believers are "Training for reigning". For example, through Paul's First Letter to the Corinthians we see that the church at Corinth was going through a rough patch with all kinds of differences rising between believers. They were threatening to take each other to the public court and Paul pleads with them not to do so. He argues that it is vital they sort out their problems within their local church, because, he says, "Do you not know that the saints will judge the world? And if the world will be judged by you, are you unworthy to judge the smallest matters? Do you not know that we shall judge angels? How much more, things that pertain to this life".

In other words, if they didn't have any training in how to make moral decisions during their lifetime, how could they one day judge the world and angels in the New Heaven and the New Earth? All kinds of administration will have to be carried out in the coming kingdom and the pressures and problems and heartaches that christians know here on earth can be turned round to train them for serving Christ in a coming day. So it has been that God has always used suffering to teach His people lessons so that they might serve Him better, not only in this life, but in the life that is to come. They are put through testing so that they might "Come forth as gold" (Job 23; 10). "Don't reject the place of your prostration", said George Matheson, "It has ever been your robing-room for royalty. Ask the great ones of the past what has been the spot of their prosperity: they will say, 'It was the cold ground on which I was lying'". Let's then ask a few great ones if this principle is true. Let's call them as witnesses.

Let's start with Abraham. Who could begin to describe the pressure Abraham felt as he climbed Mount Moriah? God had promised Abraham that through his son Isaac, all the world is going to be blessed. For long years Abraham has trusted God for the birth of Isaac and, through a miracle, Isaac came. Now God is about to test Abraham's faith by asking that he sacrifice his son. How could God keep his word and let Isaac die? How could the childless Isaac die and the promise still stand of a nation to be founded through him that would be as innumerable as stars and sand?

Scripture later tells us how Abraham got through this time of suffering that tested his faith. We read that he accounted "That God was able to raise him up, even from the dead" (Hebrews 11; 19). He believed that God was perfectly capable of resurrecting the body of Isaac.

It is no easy journey that Abraham makes up Mount Moriah and what parent could not identify with the heart-wrenching question of Isaac as he asks, "My father .... behold the fire and the wood; but where is the lamb for a burnt offering?" Yet, Abraham's faith held; he calculated on God's being able to supply all his need. God's stores of supply are inexhaustible and as the very blade of Abraham's knife flashes in the rays of the sun, the voice of an angel from Heaven cries, "Do not lay your hand on the lad or do anything to him; for now I know that you fear God since you have not withheld your son, your only son, from me".

What did Abraham call the name of the place of his testing? He called it "Jehovah-jireh" meaning "The Lord will provide". Abraham finds a ram caught by his horns in a thicket and as it is sacrified in the place of Isaac, he is taught the great doctrine of substitution. As he leaves the mountain brow of his suffering, Abraham hears the voice of God; "By myself I have sworn, says the Lord, because you have done this thing, and have not withheld your son, your only son, in blessing I will bless you, and in multiplying I will multiply your descendents as the stars of the heaven and as the sand which is on the seashore; and your descendents shall possess the gates of their enemy.

In your seed all the nations of the earth shall be blessed, because you have obeyed my voice" (Genesis 22; 16-18). Ask Abraham and he would tell you that suffering can be very productive.

Let's try another. Let's ask Joseph if the truth of blessings coming through buffetings is true. Let's break into his story when his father Jacob sends the seventeen year old Joseph to Shechem to find out how his brothers are. Little did Jacob think that as Joseph left him to go to Shechem, he would not see his son again for twenty-two years. Poor Joseph! The Scripture speaks of a man finding Joseph wandering in a field at Shechem. Can you see him there in that field, unable to find his brothers and maybe, in his heart, wishing he wouldn't. Enthusiasm is always easier than obedience but Joseph obeys his father. Obedience, though it brought Joseph much suffering, actually eventually brought incalculable reward.

Joseph eventually found his brothers who immediately wanted to kill him. By the intervention of his brother, Reuben, Joseph is put in a pit. As

Joseph lies in the pit do you think he shouts, "Praise the Lord, don't you fellows know I am to be governor of Egypt and am going to free you one day from death and starvation? This pit is marvellous because it is the actual highway of God's guidance for me!"? I am quite sure Joseph thought no such thing. He thought he was merely doing his duty and I am sure, wondered why on earth he was suffering for it. In fact he made a strong protest against the treatment he was receiving (see Genesis 42: 21).

No part of any suffering in our lives appears to be the path to blessing. Joseph in the pit looks broken beyond repairing. Gone is the coat of distinction, gone is home support, gone is every visible means of hope. But God has a purpose in it all; God does not bring good out of evil but He does bring good in spite of evil. All things that happen to us are not necessarily good, but they work together for good; His promise can be trusted. If God wants you out of where you are, He will take you out. You don't need to know key people, you just need to know the one who holds the keys. God can use just whatever He chooses to accomplish His will for you. A stalled sun for Joshua. A fleece for Gideon. A jawbone for Samson. A floating axe-head for Elisha. A lump of figs for Hezekiah. A raised golden sceptre for Esther. A burning coal for Isaiah. A great fish for Jonah. A coin in a fish's mouth for Peter. A blinding light for Paul.

The pit for Joseph was God's highway to saving a nation and preserving the line for the Messiah. Joseph goes on to bear his suffering with great dignity via the prison house and on to the governorship of Egypt. He showed sterling qualities under all the pressure. Here is ability without instability. Here is attractiveness without vanity. Here is cheerfulness without lightness. Here is gift without lording. Here is courage without rough handling. Here is godliness that is as real to the man as breathing. Here is someone who did not wait for some great occasion but who made every occasion great. Suffering is very productive in Joseph's life.

My next witness is Moses; he didn't even have to wait for suffering to begin in his teenage years. Moses' suffering lay around him in his infancy. What is that ark of bulrushes floating in the Nile? It contains the little baby Moses hidden from the murderous edict of Pharaoh who wanted every male Hebrew infant slain. If you had talked to the mighty Moses of later years, he would have dated his fortune from his danger in the Nile that day. Pharaoh's daughter, accompanied by a team of maidens, comes down to the bank of the river to bathe and seeing the ark sends her maid to get it . Now, mark this. When Pharaoh's daughter opened the lid of the ark, she saw the baby Moses and, we are told, "The babe wept, so she had compassion on him". The entire destiny of a nation hung on that little baby's tears!

Those tears moved a heart to bring up Moses in Pharaoh's palace and led the way to the most famous exodus in history. Suffering was certainly an intrusion into the lives of the Hebrew people, but it led to great blessing.

My next witness is Ruth. If you and I had happened, by chance, to come walking past two women called Ruth and Naomi standing by the border of Moab and Israel, we would probably have walked on. Just two women talking by the side of the road, the wind blowing up dust as usual, the sun pouring down on the quiet countryside at the time of barley harvest. Yet, things are never as they seem. In the heart of Ruth there struggled the biggest decision in her young life. Recently widowed, she was deciding to leave Moab to help her mother-in-law who was returning, after much suffering in her life, to Bethlehem, in Israel. Ruth had discovered the true God and was she going back to the worldly substitutes in Moab that never satisfy? Before her lies the loneliness of an alien land, the hard back-breaking work of a gleaner and a future that seems terribly blank.

Ruth made a very clear decision and declares to her mother-in-law, "Your God shall be my God". Though it meant much personal suffering, Ruth went to Bethlehem and became King David's great-grandmother. From her family line came the Saviour of the world. She may have seemed peculiar to her friends but better a thousand times effective peculiarity than uneffective ordinariness. Her complete subordination to a single aim was absolute. The end, though, lay far from gleaning alien corn. It meant an eternal spiritual harvest.

The end, as Amy Carmichael wrote, it will explain:

"Will not the end explain
The crossed endeavour, earnest purpose foiled.
The strange bewilderment of good work spoiled,
The clinging weariness, the inward strain,
Will not the end explain?

Meanwhile He comforteth
Them that are losing patience. 'Tis His way:
But none can write the words they hear Him say
For men to read; only they know He saith
Sweet words and comforteth.

Not that He doth explain
The mystery that baffleth; but a sense
Husheth the quiet heart, that far, far hence
Lieth a field set thick with golden grain
Wetted in seedling days by many a rain:
The end - it will explain."

My final Bible witness is a New Testament couple. They were called Aquila and Priscilla. This christian couple, tentmakers by trade, were absolutely devoted to one another. Here were a couple who had everything going for them: they were living in Rome and rich in love. But, suddenly, the clouds began to gather on the horizon of their happiness. There were riots in the streets of the Jewish colony across the Tiber and the cause was that old chestnut of Jewish discord, "Who was the Messiah?".

Aquila, who was a Jew, and his wife remained faithful to Christ but, along with many others, faced fanatical opposition. Whispers began to pass around the imperial court that there was a seditious movement about. "Another king, one Jesus". So it was not very difficult for the Emperor to issue a short Act ordering the immediate deportation of all Jews.

For Aquila and Priscilla it meant financial disaster because every Roman soldier carried a tent on his back when on a campaign, and Rome was the great centre for the Roman army. Some of the Jews evaded the order and hid in the slums, but Aquila and Priscilla were loyal to the order of their earthly Sovereign and moved to Corinth.

Perhaps there is someone reading this little book who has been forced to move from their town, village or city to another place. You think God has forgotten you. It is not so. Let the example of God's dealings with this couple be a starlight of encouragement to you.

Aquila and Priscilla were not only devoted to each other, they were also devoted to the servants of Christ. After they had been in Corinth for some time, Paul came to the city. He was lonely and his Athenian mission had been less promising than he had hoped. He was not well supplied with funds and the finger of God's providence led him to Aquila and Priscilla's place of business for he, like them, was a tentmaker by trade. There grew up between this trio a loyal devotion to one another which made a deep impression on Paul's mind (See Romans 16; 3-4). For eighteen months, life passed busily and then they moved, under the call of God, to Ephesus. Here, Priscilla and Aquila earned more money and had a large business - room consecrated for christian worship, because there were no public places of worship for christians.

It was here the Ephesian christians gathered, here that Timothy learned more of Christ and here that Apollos, the great scholar and orator from Alexandria was taught the Gospel by this godly couple, and Apollos became one of the greatest servants of Christ in New Testament days. (See Acts 18: 24-26).

Devoted to each other, and to the truth of God, Paul said of Aquila and Priscilla: "Not only I but all the churches of the Gentiles are grateful to them" (Romans 16: 3-4). What an inspiration they are to us today!

Despite having to move their business because of a nasty government edict, and despite all the personal suffering that came to them as a result, Aquila and Priscilla were mightily used by God to be in the vanguard for the establishment of the New Testament church. Their suffering was so productive it was to influence millions.

Let's take a few witnesses from life in general.

Who, in history, composed our greatest symphonies? Beethoven, Handel, Schubert, Chopin, Schuman, Debussy, Tchaikovsky and Dvorak are amongst our greatest composers. A look at their lives is a very illuminating experience; a little research leaves the researcher gasping. Beethoven spent his youth in poverty and misery.

As he grew older he was generally referred to as an ugly man. Tragedy of tragedies for Beethoven, he went stone deaf. It was a terrible thing to happen to a musician, and yet it was after this that he wrote some of his most wonderful music - music which he never heard himself. He never stopped producing masterpieces; 9 symphonies, 32 piano sonatas, 16 string quartets amongst a list of other works. The last twelve years of his life were lonely and unhappy and after four months of intense suffering from lung inflammation he died in December 1827 in the midst of a thunderstorm.

Handel first had to play the clavichord in an attic in case his father discovered him! Later in life, after many adventures, he composed his most widely popular work "The Messiah" under a cloud of misfortune and bitter disappointment. His last two operas had failed, largely through the plots of opponents who even hired ruffians to prevent people reaching the building where the operas were being performed. Later in life Handel went blind but he refused to give in, playing from memory and giving sound to the endless and wonderful music passing through his mind.

Schubert was, they say, a physically squat, stout, clumsy little man with an unhealthy complexion and rounded shoulders. Yet, music simply poured out of him. Chopin was plagued with ill health all his life and he had to fight constantly against disease. In later years his life was one long struggle against consumption. It was said, "He came into the room bent double and with a distressing cough ... but when he sat down to the piano he played with extraordinary strength and animation." He died at the age of 39.

Ilyich Tchaikovsky had moods that alternated between happy exuberant spirits and black depression. (Who of us hasn't?) He married a girl whom he did not love because he was afraid she would commit suicide if he refused her. After nine weeks they separated and Tchaikovsky suffered such mental torture he became unconscious. Although he said he was "worn out" and "done for", he was conceiving in his mind the haunting and beautiful "Pathetique" Symphony. He unfortunately drank some unboiled water which brought about a fatal attack of cholera.

The story is no different in many other fields of worthy endeavour. The blind Milton wrote the classic "Paradise Lost". The childhood suffering of Charles Dickens produced "David Copperfield". Robert Louis Stevenson showed no trace of the boredom of an invalid's life in "Treasure Island". Livingstone opened Africa through unbelievable personal suffering.

What shall we say of the Pilgrim Fathers setting out to found the "New World"? Were there not many tears in the process? Yet, in all of these examples suffering was productive.

We have covered a fair bit of ground since we first set out to investigate the question of suffering from a Biblical standpoint. Does the Bible, then, give us a clear-cut answer to human suffering? I would have to say that I don't really think it gives us so much a clear-cut answer to suffering as it gives us a clear-cut way to go through it. When Paul asked God three times to remove his "Thorn in the flesh", he was not told why he was suffering, but he was told by God that "My grace is sufficient for you and My strength is made perfect in weakness". It is here, then, that I rest my case. Though we may not always know why we suffer, we are promised liberating, thrilling, revolutionary, amazing, enabling grace to get us through our suffering, if we trust God through it all.

Another thing is also absolutely sure; incalculable blessing always lies at the end. "This present suffering", says the Bible, "is not to be compared with the glory that shall follow". I leave you with one final story. It could, maybe, only happen in Northern Ireland, but it certainly happened to me. I had been preaching God's Word in South Korea and developed, while there, a huge swelling. I went, on returning home to Northern Ireland, to see a doctor friend of mine who is also a christian. "Are you worried?", he asked with a twinkle in his eye when I entered his surgery and explained my problem. "Worried!", I replied, "I am frightened out of my mind!". "Well, you are not going to die then," he said. "How's that?", I asked. "Because if you were going to die, you would get dying grace, wouldn't you? Since you obviously haven't got it, you're not going to die, yet!". I thought him somewhat comfortless at the time but after the last twenty years of life's experiences, I have found he spoke more comforting truth than I could have ever imagined.

REFERENCES

1. 'Where is God When it Hurts?' by Philip Yancey.
2. 'Surprised by Joy', C. S. Lewis, Inspirational Press, New York.
3. 'The Cross of Christ', J.R.W. Stott, Inter-Varsity Press.

Guidance

**BIBLICAL DIRECTION FOR
LIFE'S CHOICES**

A survey was conducted recently in decision-making and the study concluded that all of us face between 300 and 17,000 decisions every day! It is a very good thing in life to get into the habit of making decisions and acting on them for it is better to be right 50% of the time and get something done than it is to get nothing done because you are afraid to be wrong! Ronald Regan tells the story of how he learned the need for decision-making, early in life. An aunt had taken him to a cobbler to have a pair of shoes made for him. "Do you want a square toe or a round toe?", asked the cobbler. Regan hummed and hawed. So the cobbler said, "Come back in a day or two and let me know what you want". A few days later the shoemaker saw Regan on the street and asked what he had decided about the shoes. "I still haven't made up my mind", the boy answered. "Very well", said the cobbler. When Regan received the shoes, he was shocked to see that one shoe had a square toe and the other had a round toe! "Looking at those shoes every day taught me a lesson", said Regan, years later. "If you don't make your own decisions, somebody else will make them for you".

Guidance, from a Biblical stand-point, is all about making good decisions. This study aims to be Scriptural, not philosophical. It will aim at a practical exposition of Divine guidance in individual human life as taught in Scripture and proved in human experience. We will see that every detail of our lives, down to the very smallest, is to God, a necessary part of a magnificent whole. We will see that the shining mystery and rich reality of Biblical teaching for each individual believer is the reality of "The Father above me; controlling all things. The Saviour beside me; directing my footsteps. The Spirit within me, impressing me inwardly". The categorical truth of Scripture is that God does still guide His people. Some decisions in our lives are small ones and some are large, but God has promised to guide and help us to make those decisions as we pass through life's labyrinth of ways. He knows the future and He alone can give us that guidance for today which safeguards tomorrow. God has a purpose for each one of us as no-one else has. This study looks at the ways He guides and leads us to know and fulfil that purpose.

I. THE THREE LIGHTS

Many years ago a famous Christian writer was travelling from an Irish port to Holyhead on the Welsh coast. He was standing on the bridge with the captain, chatting to him about the voyage. "How do you know when you are on course for Holyhead?", he asked him. "When I approach the port", replied the captain, "I see three lights on the horizon. When I manoeuvre my ship to a position where I can make the three lights, one light, I am on course for Holyhead". The Christian writer lifted his pen when he got home and wrote of how Christians have three lights which are always on the horizon of their lives to guide them. When they find those three lights are one light, they can be sure they are on course for making a good decision in their lives within the will of God. The first light is the light of the Scriptures. If the Scriptures are against what you are going to do, then don't do it. They have spoken out clearly on a multitude of issues from marriage to communication, from neighbourhood relations to handling enemies, from running a business to life's true priorities, from being a good parent to finding the way to Heaven. If the Scriptures have spoken clearly and directly on an issue, then we need no further guidance on the issue; we simply obey the Scriptures.

There are, of course, other things on which the Scriptures have not spoken clearly. They have not told us, for example, whether to go to Portavogie or Portugal for our holidays, have they? They have not told us whether to wear blue socks or red socks, today. They have not told us which specific person to marry or not to marry. They have not spelled out which particular house to buy or not to buy, which particular flat to rent or which college or university to study in, or what particular job to take or refuse. In such situations, God uses another light on the horizon of the believer's life, the light of circumstance. Suddenly we find ourselves in a particular circumstance and wonder what on earth is going on. Our very lives at times may seem to be caving in and it almost appears as if God has forgotten us. Do you not think Joseph wondered what God was up to when his brothers threw him in a pit? Do you think, had you been talking to him, he would have said, "It's wonderful down here, I am on my way to becoming Prime Minister of Egypt?". Do you think as his brothers sold him to the Ishmeelites who took him as a slave to Egypt that he had any idea that the day would come when Pharaoh would say to Joseph, "Without your consent no man may lift his hand or foot in all the land of Egypt"?

As Joseph entered into prison because a very evil woman had lied about him, he did not know that the prison was God's highway to the palace! Circumstances in our lives are often dark, but, if we only realised it, they are God's light in the path of guidance to lead us on to the next important phase of our lives. The Scripture tells us that "On the first day of the week Mary Magdalene came to the tomb early, while it was still dark". She found the Saviour's tomb, empty, and thought it was the darkest day of her life. Frantically she went searching for His body, telling Peter in despair of what had happened. She even found a man that she thought was the gardener and said, "Sir, if you have carried Him away, tell me where you have laid Him and I will come and take Him away". Superbly, of course, what Mary thought was the darkest day of her life turned out to be the best day of her life. In fact, it turned out to be the best day in the history of the entire world. The supposed gardener turned out to be the risen Christ! The greatest news the world ever heard came out of a graveyard!

Don't, then, panic when circumstances seem to threaten. God uses circumstances as a light to guide you. Yet, on their own, circumstances as a guide can be dangerous. Jonah, the rebellious prophet, found his circumstances very conducive. The wind was in the right direction. The ship's captain was amiable. Jonah had money in his pocket. He said, in effect, "Viva, España!" and set sail for the Spanish coast. Circumstances looked fine but the Word of the Lord had already told Jonah to go to Nineveh. It took very frightening circumstances to arise in order to bring

Jonah to see that when God guides us, the light of circumstances and the light of His Word must be one before we set sail on a new phase of our lives. The third light is the light of the "Peace of God". There is a great difference between "Peace with God" and the "Peace of God". When a person receives Christ as Saviour, they are justified by faith and immediately have "Peace with God through our Lord Jesus Christ". That means they are no longer at enmity with God, they are now at peace with Him. All hell cannot remove a person from that position. "The Peace of God", though, is different. It is conditional. "In everything, by prayer and supplication with thanksgiving, let your requests be made known to God and the peace of God which surpasses all understanding will guard your hearts and minds through Christ Jesus", says the Bible.

When Christians request something from God with a thankful heart for what God has already given them, then the "Peace of God", the tranquillity of God's own eternal being, the peace which God Himself has, the calm serenity that characterises His very nature, will become theirs. Yet, we must always remember, it is conditional. It comes by prayer and an attitude of thankfulness. God's peace is able to produce better results than human planning and is more effective for removing anxiety than any intellectual effort or power of reasoning. It "rises above every mind". It will protect the Christian's heart and mind, i.e. the Christian's entire inner being; emotions, affections, thoughts, and, vitally important, all their moral choices. This is what Christians mean when they say, "Do you have peace about it?". They mean does a sense of the peace of God fill your mind and heart about what you are going to decide to do in a given circumstance. Even if the whole world is shoving you to do something, if you do not have a sense of the peace of God about what you are going to do, don't let them budge you.

So it is that when faced with a decision in life, a Christian must make sure that the light of the Word of God, the light of circumstance, and the light of the peace of God, are one light. If one of these three is missing, wait until it comes into line and then proceed. You will find that God's lights of guidance, if followed, will never lead you on to the rocks. Trust Him.

2. ARE YOU UP-TIGHT ABOUT GUIDANCE?

Despite the lights of guidance that God provides along the voyage of life, a lot of people are very up-tight about knowing God's will in their lives. In fact many are full of fear and guilt on the subject. Why? It all stems from the fact that they think they have missed the will of God for their lives. You know the type; "God called me to go up the Amazon as a missionary when I was twenty-two but I didn't go and now the rest of my Christian life is a failure". There is another fear many Christians experience. It is not that they have deliberately disobeyed God's call, it is that they fear they have, unintentionally, misread it. They fear they have an innate lack of ability to read God's signs of guidance correctly. J.I. Packer puts it very well when he likens our fears about guidance to thinking that God's plan for our lives is like an itinerary drawn up by a travel agent. As long as we follow the agent's instructions and be in the right place, at the right time, boarding each aircraft, bus or boat as indicated, then all is well. But miss one of the pre-planned connections and the itinerary is ruined.

A revised plan can only be second-best compared with the original programme. Is this your view of God's will for your life? Is this your view of God? If you miss a connection here or there along the way, do you really think God cannot bring you back to His purpose for you? Have you forfeited your usefulness? Let me ask if you would treat your own child in such a manner? I doubt it very much. Why then do you think your Heavenly Father, who is love itself, would treat you, His child, differently? Let's look at some characters in Scripture who made a mess of things regarding the will of God in their lives. It is a fascinating meditation. Take Abraham, for an example. Abraham panicked on the path of God's will and fled to Egypt, lying to Pharaoh that Sarah his wife was his sister to protect himself. God had given Abraham great promises that He would guide and direct him but he forgot about those promises and lived on his wits. He was thrown out of Egypt by Pharaoh. What hope would you have given that Abraham would become a legend and an inspiration in history, as a man of staggering faith in God? None! Yet, he did become just that. God got him back on track and he became known as the Father of the Faithful.

Think about Moses. A meditation on the life of Moses, after murdering an Egyptian in order, he thought, to further God's cause will not lead you to the conclusion that God made sure he became a second rate leader because of his disastrous mistake. He became one of the greatest leaders in all of history.

What do you make of the con-man Jacob? Manipulative, supplanting, self-centred Jacob made sure, by foul means, that things went his way. Look at what God did through him; he became a "Prince" with God. His disastrous beginning did not ensure a disastrous end.

Could we have a greater example in all of Scripture of a person who, despite much error, eventually fulfilled the will of God for his life than Samson? Quite frankly, Samson disobeyed virtually every rule in God's book. Yet, the angel told his mother that he would "Begin to deliver Israel from the Philistines". Did he?

What is your view of Samson? A big lout? A he-man with a she-weakness? A man who fooled about with God's gifts to him and who was eventually discarded by God? This is not God's ultimate view. He certainly did deliberately disobey God's instructions to him on many occasions but for many years I reckon about twenty he judged Israel successfully. His failures are highlighted by God for our learning, but, when Samson died, he effected a greater deliverance from the enemies of God's people by his death than even by his life!

There was no doubt that the enemies of God eventually knew where Samson's strength originated. He got back on track, all right, with a vengeance!

Did Peter not disobey God's will for his life? Most certainly. He denied to a teenage girl that he even knew the Christ. He who had said he would die for the Saviour miserably failed to live for Him on the night when the Saviour needed him most. Was he thrown aside by the Lord? Did be become a God's second-best Christian?

Have you read any of Peter's New Testament letters recently? There are fewer passages of Scripture more inspiring for people going through trouble. Was he restored to God's purpose for his life? Fewer have known a more complete restoration. A few weeks later he was leading thousands to faith in Christ. The Saviour met Peter by the lake, warmed him by a fire and fed him with fish and pointed him to the way back. Peter discovered that neither his sin, nor his temper or mood, nor the passage of time had lessened Christ's love for him nor dampened Christ's desire to see Peter live out God's purposes for his life.

So, Christian, if you have made a bad decision or sinned in disobeying God's clear instructions to you, it is categorically not the end. God knew that you and I were failures before He took us on. He has promised never to leave us nor forsake us, no matter who else does. As He told the erring Abraham, "I am your shield and your exceeding great reward". God loves us and is not going to put us on the scrap-heap or the shelf just because we have erred. It is true that sin has its earthly consequences and that stupid and silly decisions have repercussions but if there is repentance on our part and a willingness to try again, God can restore and use us.

Let me sign out this chapter with a more modern example of what we are thinking about. A wild, dissolute and drunken youth went one evening to a home Bible study amongst a few Christians in Germany. He got converted to Christ. Fervent in his faith but pretty empty in Scriptural knowledge he thought that God wanted him to be a missionary. Having a knowledge of betting on horses he went to a racecourse and put a bet on a horse. "If it wins, Lord", he prayed, "I will know you want me to be a missionary!". If you had been passing that racecourse you wouldn't have given much hope for that young man ever finding God's will in his life, would you?

His name was George Muller and he became one of the greatest Christians in British history! Selah.

So, quit being up-tight about guidance. Admit your mistakes, repent if you have been disobedient and sinful and trust in the Lord with all your heart, lean not to your own understanding, in all your ways acknowledge Him and He shall direct your paths.

3. OBEYING STANDING ORDERS

A lot of people think of Divine guidance in terms of special Divine intervention in the life of a Christian every time he or she has a major decision to make. Is such a view scriptural? Does God intervene every time we have to make decisions?

Let's take it on the human level, first. Parents in training children do not intervene in every decision their children make in life, do they? Certainly not. Why? Because if they did, their children would never grow up. They would never learn to make responsible decisions later in life if they were not given freedom to make some earlier in life. A parent intervening all the time would create a very spoiled child bereft of social skills needed for balanced living. Such an approach would also create a child who would be eventually seriously flawed in any decision-making process in their life.

What would any wise parent do in order to aid their child to be a good decision-maker? They would set their child limits to observe. Obviously a child would not be allowed to do whatever it wanted because, out of lack of experience for a start, it might choose a line of action whose consequences the child would simply not be capable of knowing. To allow it complete freedom would bring incalculable disaster. Yet, drawing from the wisdom of his parents and their example, and observing the limits set, a child can be allowed freedom to make decisions.

By such a process the child slowly but surely grows up to be a responsible adult.

Let's take these guidelines to the spiritual level. God wants His children to grow up responsibly. He wants them to be able to use their minds and exercise their spiritual muscles and make good decisions in their lives. Though, He too sets limits to observe. The Bible shows very clearly what God hates to see in His image-bearers. So we, by His grace, can avoid those things that God hates. Drawing, then, from God's wisdom and observing the limits He sets as revealed in the Scriptures and having His example to follow as reflected in the life of the Lord Jesus while He was here on earth, we are allowed to use our minds to make good decisions and so grow up as responsible Christians.

There is, in Scripture, a very gripping and instructive example of those principles we have just been thinking about. It concerns a very important pivot in the history of the Christian church, namely, the story of how Paul was guided to first bring the Gospel of Jesus Christ to Europe.

Consider the scene. God wants to bring Paul to Europe to sow a very important seed whose harvest we are enjoying today. Did He intervene in Paul's life with a flash of lightning from the sky or have some Scripture verse burden him heavily to shift him from the Middle East to Europe? Not on this occasion.

We simply read in Acts 15; 36 that "After some days Paul said to Barnabas, 'Let us now go back and visit our brethren in every city where we have preached the Word of the Lord and see how they are doing' ".

What were Paul and Barnabas doing? They were simply responding to God's standing order that shepherds of God's flock should care for and feed their sheep. Paul and Barnabas needed no special guidance for that any more than Germans need a letter from their Chancellor, or the British need a letter from their Queen or Americans need a letter from their President every week to tell them to pay their taxes! As a friend of mine once put it, "What mother, in normal circumstances, would earnestly pray to the Lord for direct special guidance whether it was His will that she give her baby its breakfast?"

The plain fact is that we don't need special Divine guidance in a whole lot of areas of activity in our lives. The standing order to the Christian is to be a good citizen, a good neighbour, to spread the Gospel, to care for family and friends, etc. So, let's get on with the standing orders, just like Paul did and if we need special intervention from God to guide us, we will get it. Paul did. As he went to encourage the churches he had planted, God intervened with special guidance, twice. Yet, notice that it was with negative intervention, telling him not to go to Asia or Bithynia. (See Acts 16; 6-7).

It is vital to understand that all of this time Paul and those friends with him were never given advance information as to where God was eventually leading them! Paul didn't know that when God stopped him going to preach in Asia and then in Bithynia that the whole purpose was to get him to go to Philippi. Moses' parents didn't get advance information that when they put their baby in an ark of bulrushes and floated it in the Nile, that Pharaoh's daughter would find the child, adopt him and that God would get Moses to eventually lead the Children of Israel across the wilderness! You don't get advance information from God that when you lose a job, or are passed over for promotion, or are sidelined by your friends through no fault of your own, that it will all lead to a wonderful goal God has for you in the future. Everything that happens to us is not necessarily good, but it always works together for good.

Special Divine guidance may not necessarily let you know where you are being led. It may be just to keep you "On track" on the line of obeying God's standing orders.

Eventually Paul and his friends arrived in Troas. We are not told how long it took them to get there but it must have been a very long journey taking up a considerable amount of time. They got special Divine guidance in the form of a vision which Paul had in the night. A man from Macedonia stood and pleaded with Paul saying, "Come over to Macedonia and help us".

Did Paul jump out of bed in the morning and say, "Right men, we are off to Europe?". He did not. He first of all talked over what he had experienced with his friends and the Scripture says that they "concluded" (i.e. inferred) that the Lord had called them to Macedonia. It is, therefore, a very good idea to discuss with Godly and caring friends those things which you consider to be special Divine guidance in your life.

Paul and his party eventually arrived in Philippi and the Lord opened Lydia's heart to the Gospel. She in turn opened her home to Paul and Silas and God in turn opened the continent of Europe to the best news it ever heard.

What do we learn, then, from this Scriptural story to help us in the nitty gritty of seeking God's guidance for our daily lives? If we were never allowed to decide anything but were always controlled by constant interventions from God directly guiding us, we would never grow up to be mature Christians.

When God's plans or our needs require it, God can and often does intervene with special guidance. This may be in the form of a dramatic intervention or may be through a circumstance such as bumping into a friend, receiving a telephone call, reading a magazine article or crossing a certain street. Great doors swing on little hinges.

God sets limits for our behaviour by showing us in the Bible the things that He hates. If we, by His grace, avoid these, our decisions within these limits will bring glory to Him and help us to mature. God never by-passes or suppresses our moral or spiritual judgment. If God broke your mind, you would be as a jelly-fish or a vegetable. He helps you by His Holy Spirit to will to do His will. When a good door closes, God opens a better one.

4. WHEN IS THE WRONG ROAD THE RIGHT ROAD?

Question: When is the wrong road, the right road?
Answer: When God sends you on it.

Here are some stories to illustrate this truth.

Some years ago, the late Bishop Taylor Smith was travelling by railway from somewhere in northern England to somewhere south. He missed a connection at Leeds, Yorkshire, and found he had two hours to wait. As always, in such circumstances, he accepted this as "permissive Providence", and prayed for guidance, asking if God had some special purpose in allowing the delay. Strolling from the station to the big square outside, he sat on a form, and noticed that its only other occupant was a middle-aged man who looked the very picture of misery. Shabbily dressed, bent shoulders, head drooped down on his hands, he took no notice whatever of the burly clergyman who now sat near him. Still counting on guidance, the Bishop said, "You seem to be in some deep trouble". "Yes, I sure am", the man muttered, without lifting his eyes. "I'm at the end of things, Mr". He coughed hoarsely, then added, "Maybe you'll not believe me, Mr, but tonight I'm going to end everything; and I'm just having this last sit out here". "But is there no-one can help you?", asked the Bishop. "Nobody", came the dejected reply.

After a pause, head sagging still lower, the man added, "Begging your pardon, stranger, there's just one man who could have helped me, if I could have found him; but I haven't seen him these fifteen years, and I have no notion where he is". "Who is he?" asked the Bishop.

"He was my army Padre in France during the war, but I clean forget his name". "Which regiment and company were you in? What battles were you in?", enquired the Bishop. The man slowly told him, still without looking up. Then, stretching out his hand, and gently lifting the man's head up, the Bishop said, "Well, my brother, look at me; your man is right here; I was that Padre; and after all these years God has sent me to help you here and now!".

Just recently a friend of mine, a mathematics lecturer at a Welsh University, missed his train connection in a European city. His colleagues were greatly perturbed by the incident but my friend contented himself with the fact that God makes no mistakes. He waited for another

connection and eventually settled down in his railway carriage. There he
got into conversation with a couple from, of all places, Siberia. He
discovered them to be vitally interested in spiritual things and happening
to have a Russian Bible in his case, offered it to them.

Their surprise was quite overwhelming. How could he know that just a
few weeks previously they had had their most precious possession stolen;
namely, their Bible. The woman hugged her new-found copy as if it were
the crown jewels!

My friend knew, then, why he had missed his connection.

Would anybody stubbornly pretend that such happenings are mere
coincidences? Surely they are the operation of real Divine guidance in
and through consecrated individuals. What channels of blessing we might
become if we were only living such guided lives! Don't think, though, that
leading such a guided life brings wonderful consequences immediately. I
love to tell the story of my good friends at Capernwray Hall, the Christian
Conference Centre and Bible School situated in its own beautiful grounds
in Lancashire, England. A while back the directors of Capernwray Hall
bought a castle in Austria as a holiday and conference centre and God
richly blessed them in their work there. They wondered why things were
so especially blessed until one day they found a Bible belonging to the
man who had built the castle. He had written a prayer on the fly-leaf of
the Bible asking God to use the castle to His glory. Though the man had
done his best to serve the Lord, holding services in the castle, and
witnessing to others, he was severely persecuted throughout his
Christian life. He died, heartbroken and with no evident results from his
faithful service. He seemed to have been on the wrong road of service.
Was he? Not at all. God answered his prayer when my friends from
Capernwray moved in. The significant thing, though, is that my friends
discovered the Bible and its written prayer to be seven hundred years old!

Are you discouraged on the path of doing what you know to be the will
of God? Have you had clear guidance and have sought all these months,
and maybe even years, to do it? Is there no great sign that you are being

successful? Who said that you were to be judged on outward success, encouraging as it is when it comes? Surely what you are called to be is to be faithful. In the end, doing God's will is good, perfect and acceptable, though, at the time you are carrying it out, it appears to be anything but scintillating.

Take Amy Carmichael, the great Christian Missionary to India. Amy set up a superb work in South India to rescue little children from being sold into temple prostitution. Hundreds were saved from this dreadful trade and, yet, one night Amy fell into a hole unlit by builders in her compound and became an invalid for thirty years. From that invalid's bed came some of the most moving and Christ-exalting Christian literature ever written, which has in turn touched millions of lives. In Switzerland, recently, to preach God's Word I came across an older Christian lady who had worked with Amy all those years ago and as we talked around her dining room table, she told me how the invalided Amy used to keep a lamp burning in her window at night. "That lamp is for you", she said, "To cheer you as you return to your bungalow from your day's labour for the Lord Jesus".

What seemed to be a devastatingly "wrong road" turned out in the over-ruling providence of God to be a road of incredible blessing. Recently a member of my Bible Class and an outstanding Christian student leader called Kirsty Noble sent me the following poem. The author is unknown but the poem is powerfully relevant to the theme we have just been talking about. I ask you to ponder these words very carefully.

> She asked to be made like her Saviour,
> And He took her at her word,
> And sent her a heart-crushing burden
> Till the depths of her soul were stirred.
> She asked for a faith strong, yet simple.
> He permitted the dark clouds to come;
> She staggered by faith through the darkness,
> As the storms did her soul o'erwhelm.

She prayed to be filled with a passion
Of love for lost souls and for God,
And again in response to her longing,
She sank 'neath the chastening rod.
She wanted a place in His vineyard;
He took her away from her home,
And placed her among hardened sinners
Where she humanly stood all alone.
She gave up all worldly ambitions,
Those "castles in air" of years.
And she knelt in deep consecration,
And whispered "Amen" through her tears.
She wanted a meek, lowly spirit -
The work He gave answered that cry;
And those who had been her companions
With pitying smile passed her by.
She asked to lean hard on her Saviour;
He took human props quite away,
Till no earthly friend could help her,
And she could do nothing but pray.
I saw her go out to the vineyard
To harvest the golden grain;
Her eyes were still moistened with weeping,
Her heart was still throbbing with pain.
But many a heart that was broken,
And many a wrecked, blighted life
Was made to thank God for her coming,
And rejoice in the midst of the strife.
She had prayed to be made like her Saviour,
And the burden He gave her to bear
Had been but the great Sculptures training;
Thus answering her earnest prayer.

5. THE ROLE OF THE BIBLE IN GUIDANCE

It constantly amazes me how few people actually read the Scriptures. In The Dark Ages, copies of the Scriptures were chained to the pulpit in the secret language of the clergy and the public were kept stone ignorant of the life-changing teaching of its truths. Men like Tyndale were then burnt alive for trying to get the Scriptures into the hands of the common people. In those days Biblical ignorance was forced. Now, in our day, it is voluntary. In fact the more versions of Scripture we have, the less the Bible is read. What I have just written, though, needs to be qualified. We need to remember that more than half the languages of the world have no portion of Scripture at all. This embraces, perhaps, one hundred and fifty million people. In many areas there are very severe restrictions on the publication and sale of the Bible. The sad fact remains, though, particularly in the western world, that when people have the Scriptures in their own language with a ready access to them and absolute freedom to study them, so few actually do in comparison with those who don't!

In a school, here in the West, a teacher quizzed a group of college-bound High School pupils on the Bible. Here are some of the answers he received;

Jesus was baptized by Moses.

Sodom and Gomorrah were lovers.

Jezreel was Ahab's donkey.

The New Testament Gospels were written by Matthew, Mark, Luther and John.

Eve was created from an apple.

The most hilarious, if sad, answer to the question,

"What was Golgotha?" was,

"Golgotha was the name of the giant who slew the Apostle David".

Despite the fact that millions neglect the Scriptures, it does not take away the reality that there is no other place where better guidance can be found for everyday living. Just recently I talked with one of my local church's elders who was off to Kiev to teach business ethics to businessmen emerging from Communism. His textbook was the book of Proverbs!

To move away from the pages of Scripture is to enter into the waste-lands of subjectivity. The Bible is a divinely provided map containing directions and markings to guide people to the true order for family or nation. To ignore its teachings leads to moral and spiritual shipwreck. I am calling, in this little study, for a return to actually reading, for at least twenty minutes each day, a portion of Scripture. No, I don't mean reading the Bible just to prepare a Sunday School class, or to prepare sermons or a talk at the local prison chapel or old-folks' homes.

I mean reading the Bible for twenty minutes every day for yourself.

Get a "One Year Bible" which divides the Scripture up into readings which will take you from Genesis to Revelation in one year. (There is even a "One Minute Bible" which will give you one minute daily readings, but, I challenge you to twenty minutes a day!). No matter where you are, no matter who you have got to meet, no matter what deadlines crop up, spend twenty minutes in the Word every day. Right? There is of course nothing magical in reading the Scriptures. They need to be obeyed and you need to know the Author, which is possible through Jesus Christ. We know very well that professional religious types have been merely reading the Scriptures and disobeying them for centuries. Even the Pharisees of Christ's day who read the Bible constantly, put the Saviour they spoke of on a cross and then went right back to reading the Scriptures again. It is obviously important that the Scriptures are obeyed and the Saviour they present, trusted. Yet, if you read the Scriptures regularly, the benefits are enormous. If you doubt me, just check out these points from Psalm 119. They spell out the benefits very clearly;

1.   God's Word establishes my way. (v.5)

2.   God's Word purifies my life. (v.9-11)

3.   God's Word gives me counsel. (v.24)

4.   God's Word removes everything false in me. (v.29)

5.   God's Word produces reverence for God. (v.38)

6.   God's Word increases my courage. (v.46)

7.   God's Word comforts me in afflictions. (v.50)

8.   God's Word guards me from panic. (v.61-62)

9.   God's Word teaches me discernment and knowledge. (v.65-66)

10.   God's Word makes me resourceful. (v.79)

11.   God's Word cultivates patience. (v.87)

12.   God's Word keeps me spiritually recharged. (v.93)

13.   God's Word accelerates my understanding. (v.98-100)

14.   God's Word creates a joyful heart. (v.111)

15.   God's Word sustains me when I feel helpless. (v.116)

16.   God's Word enables me to honour what is right and hate what is wrong. (v.128)

17.   God's Word causes me to walk in the truth. (v.133)

18.   God's Word surrounds me with delight in spite of difficulty. (v.143)

19. God's Word develops the discipline of prayer. (v.147)

20. God's Word rescues me when I am defenceless. (v.152-154)

21. God's Word fills me with praise without and peace within. (v.164-165)

22. God's Word draws me back when I stray. (v.176)

It is a fact that nothing else will do for me what the Scriptures will. It is vital that we make place for them in our daily lives. As for helping us in our decision-making, which, we have discovered is the main thrust of guidance, there is a grid of some Biblical principles and some checkpoints which together constitute the way of wisdom for all who follow the Lord. These have been helpfully listed by J. I. Packer. So, then, when we have a decision to make, let us, remember:

1. THERE ARE INSTRUCTIONS TO HEED

There is obviously no point in asking God for guidance if we refuse to obey the instructions He has already given in the Scriptures. For example, the Scriptures say that "If I regard iniquity in my heart the Lord will not hear me". (Psalm 66; 18). This means that if I hug grudges, enjoy tittle-tattle, nurse jealousies, pass on gossip, lead an undisciplined, self-indulgent life, I disqualify myself from heart-to-heart fellowship with Christ and hold back guidance. If I obey the instructions in God's Word, I will find God's Will, if I disregard them, I won't.

Ninety percent of knowing God's Will is, of course, being willing to do it before I even know what it is!

2. THERE ARE LIMITS TO OBSERVE

If I deliberately step beyond the limits God puts down in His Word for me, I will stray from His Will. The Lord Jesus said that the Christian walk would take us on what He described as a "narrow way." That narrow way does not get any wider the longer I am on it, does it? It will be narrow right to the end. There will be kerb-stones and fences, limits set to where I can walk. The "broad way", on the other hand, "which leads to destruction", has not got the same limits. On the broad way I can by and large say what I like, think what I like, behave how I like and, I can carry what baggage I like. The choice is mine. If I want to walk the narrow way which leads to life, I must observe the limits it sets.

3. THERE ARE EXAMPLES TO FOLLOW

There is nothing quite like Scripture to show me examples of men and women finding and doing God's Will in their lives. From the butler Nehemiah to the gleaner, Ruth; from the shepherd boy David to the fig-picker, Amos; from the intellectual Daniel to the little servant girl in the house of Naaman; from the garment-making Dorcas to the tent-making Paul, all found God's guidance and did His Will.

You and I can follow their example.

4. THERE IS WISDOM TO DRAW ON

I refer, in part, to the book of Proverbs. This book has a lot to say about the issues of life. Here is instruction for young people in a world where subtle and restless efforts are made to poison their hearts and pervert their ways. Here are verbal gold vaults of wisdom for parents raising a family. Here are words of advice for those who are unemployed and living from hand to mouth. Here is incisive warning about the power of speech. Here you will read wisdom regarding anger, education, food, drink, justice, greed, self-control, the place of a woman and the place of a man in society and much more.

To sum up our Biblical approach to guidance, here are ten checkpoints to help when we are seeking God's Will in any situation;

1. Ask the question; "What is the best I can do for my God in this situation?".

2. Note the instructions of Scripture; on many issues the Bible has already spoken.

3. Follow the examples of Godliness in Scripture. Imitate the love and humility of Jesus Himself.

4. Let wisdom judge the best course of action; the question we should ask is no longer; "What is God's Will?"; instead the question is; "How do I make good decisions?"

5. Always note nudges from God that come your way; special burdens of concern or restlessness of heart might indicate that something needs to be changed.

6. Cherish the Divine peace that Paul says, "garrisons" the hearts of those who are in God's Will.

7. Observe the limits set by circumstances to what is possible. When it is clear those limits cannot be changed, accept them as from God.

8. Be prepared for God's guidance to be withheld until the right time comes for a decision. God usually guides one step at a time.

9. Be prepared for God to direct you to something you do not like, and teach you to like it!

10. Never forget that if you make a bad decision, it is not the end. God forgives and restores.

Thank you so much for reading this study and it is our prayer that you may experience the joy of knowing God's Will in your life. Ninety percent of knowing God's Will is, of course, being ready to do it even before He reveals it to you. Are you ready?

Oh, to be always ready,
To do Thy perfect Will;
Alert for every challenge
Thy purpose to fulfil!
Ready with fervent daring
In holy war for Thee;
Ready for burden-bearing
If that Thy Will should be.
Oh, to be always ready
To go or to obey,
A "vessel unto honour",
"Prepared" and "Sanctified"!
Ready for witness-bearing,
Though stumbling, truly wise,
Ready for sorrow-sharing,
To soothe and sympathise.
Oh, to be always ready,
To serve without applause,
Forgiving, calm and steady,
If blamed without a cause;
Ready by daily lingerings,
In Thine own Word and prayer;
Ready, at last for Heaven,
To meet and serve Thee there.

- J. Sidlow Baxter

Values

THINGS WORTH
STANDING UP FOR

To say that values are falling apart in our generation is an understatement. Everything seems to be relative in our day, nothing seems to be absolute. To find someone with a value system and to see them stick to it is rare in our generation. In education, in science, in politics, in the home, in the judiciary, one could be forgiven for believing that rules seem to be based on the question, "What can it do for me?"

Selfishness seems to rule under the maxim; "Look after Number One". Our generation is the generation of the zapper; the person who moves from T.V. channel to T.V. channel after the three minute boredom threshold has been exhausted. This generation, said Michael Ignatiff, has "The attention span of a flea". Self-centredness and shallowness is widespread and what T.S. Elliott said about his generation is even more relative to ours; he spoke of, "The hollow men".

Recently when I was trying to hold up a Biblical value system on a B.B.C. programme which included on its panel a Marxist, a Social Worker, and a South African University Lecturer, the Moderator of the programme accused me of "Living on the Planet Zob". Some of my fellow-panellists held out strongly that there can be no such thing as a shared value system for human beings.

In this study I want to maintain that there is a value system which is worth following and in which we can all share. I want to draw your attention to the character of Daniel living out his life in ancient Babylon according to a value system from which we can draw deep inspiration for our everyday living. I gratefully acknowledge the help of my friend, Professor David Gooding, who first gave me a key to the understanding of the value system that Daniel followed. It is, in fact, God's value system and it is unbeatable for true success, wholesome living and leads to the blessing of any individual who follows it.

1. VALUES IN APPETITE

Our study in values begins in the fabulous city of ancient Babylon. Here is a city occupying an area of two hundred square miles and is built on both sides of the Euphrates. It is protected by a double defensive wall reinforced with towers. To the outside of this wall, about twenty yards distant, is an additional defence wall of burnt brick set in bitumen. Access to the city is gained by eight gates, the most impressive of which is the Isthar gate. To reach it you have to pass down part of the great stone paved processional street which is about a thousand yards in length. It is decorated on either side with figures of lions in enamelled brick. Assyrian art is at its height at this period and the draftsmanship and execution of these animals indicates an advanced degree of artistic skill. There are some fifty temples within the city of Babylon.

In the midst of all this complex is situated one of the seven wonders of the world, the celebrated Hanging Gardens of Babylon. They consist of terraces supported on huge masonry arches, on which carefully tended gardens have been laid out at different levels. The interesting feature of these raised gardens is the fact that they are visible above the tops of the buildings, and provide a welcome contrast of greenery against an otherwise unrelieved background of white roofs or an expansive sky. A number of mechanical hoists provide the means by which water is raised to these elevated terraces.

In an enclosed area south west of the Isthar gate is the huge Ziggurat of Babylon which was closely linked with the Temple of Marduk in the time of Nebuchadnezzar. The Marduk shrine was by far the most ornate, being richly decorated with gold, alabaster, cedar wood panelling, and semi-precious stones. In all, Babylon at its height was the most splendid city of the world.

In the middle of all this is a young ex-patriot Jew who rises, with three of his friends, to a position of great prominence. He is a man of prayer who is not ashamed to believe what the Scriptures teach regarding the coming Age of Peace which will be brought by the Messiah. Even though Jerusalem was wrecked and he is an exile, he goes right on believing the Scriptures. The Temple might be demolished in Jerusalem, Nebuchadnezzar might hold him and his three friends captive in Babylon, but God through His prophet Isaiah has promised that He will bring Israel back from her seventy year exile in Babylon. Daniel believes God, even though there is precious little sign of His promise being fulfilled as he lives out his life.

We too can be like Daniel. Our Saviour and Messiah has promised to return to this earth of ours. Do we go on believing His promise even though our contemporaries mock us, saying "Where is the sign of His coming?". The promises of God are the foundation of God's value system. Though the earth itself should change, the mountains tumble and swirling floods rage, God, the Lord of Hosts always keeps His promises. Hitch your life to them and you won't be sorry.

Daniel and his three friends soar to the top in their exams in the University of Babylon. They do not just study the Bible, they are experts in the Chaldean language and literature and one day, right in the context of their education, they take their first stand for God's value system. They refuse to eat the food placed before them.

It all had to do with Jewish food laws. There were three areas where food was unclean to the Jew according to the Mosaic Law. There were clean and unclean animals. To eat unclean animals was to eat unclean food. Had it to do with hygiene? No, for Christ cancelled the Old Testament food laws for the christian and Paul stated that everything is to be received if it be received with thanksgiving. That certainly did not mean that pigs had become more hygienic in New Testament than in Old Testament days!

The whole purpose of this law was that it was symbolic. God was Holy and He expected His people to be holy. The physical rule of not eating certain foods was to teach His people deeper lessons. God was saying that there are some ways of satisfying our appetites that are unclean. Just look around you in our generation and see what has happened in the area of sexual appetite. A sexual appetite is perfectly healthy in itself and when expressed within the bounds God has put for it in His Word, it is obviously one of His greatest gifts to us. Yet when that appetite is fed in an unclean way, look at what happens. What are the subjects dealt with by most films and novels in our generation? They deal with rapists, adulterers, sadists, homosexuals, and every kind of sexual perversion on the face of the earth. You couldn't have a more unclean feeding of your sexual appetite than that which most video shops present.

Look at the area of the appetite of thirst. Millions are spent by the drinks industry to advertise alcohol with its subsequent social and domestic disasters. What is even dished up to our generation in certain areas of ballet and other aesthetic arts is anything but healthy for us.

It was also commanded of the Jewish people that they refuse all food offered to idols. Underlying this commandment was the question of loyalty to God. So it was that Daniel took very seriously the question of how he fed his appetites and where his loyalty lay. There was no mistaking it, though, that when Daniel and his friends said, "No" to the king's food, they were asking for their very lives to be taken.

What is the practical application of what Daniel and his friends did for our day and generation? The application is that Christians too must show that they are different by taking a stand for the wholesome feeding of their appetites. It does not mean that they are not to use their minds, though, does it? It was in the context of his education that Daniel took his stand for the wholesome feeding of his appetite. So Christians in our generation are not to be anti-intellectual and they must know that the mind matters in God's value system. Why? Because:

- We were created to think. (Psalm 32: 9; Jeremiah 8: 7).

- We will be judged by our knowledge and our response to God's revelation. (Jeremiah 25: 3, 4; John 12: 48).

- We need our minds in worship. (I Corinthians 14: 13-19).

- We need our minds to exercise faith. (Matthew 6: 26).

- The mind is vital in the quest for holiness. (Romans 12: 2).

- The mind is vital in the preaching of the Gospel. (I Timothy 4: 13-16).

- The mind matters in pastoral care as a shepherd seeks to feed the flock of God. (Proverbs 2: 1-6).

We are facing idolatry today as great as Daniel and his friends faced in the days when the Babylonians worshipped their god, Marduk. We must rise up and oppose it with our intellects and in the name of morality with God's help. Never forget that the young men who took their stand for God in Babylon were no intellectual slouches. Let's follow their lead and example.

2. VALUES IN SCIENCE

We desperately need, in our generation, to bring our minds to bear upon one of the greatest challenges to our faith; it is the challenge that our contemporaries bring which says that science and the Bible are incompatible. We want to maintain that true science and the Bible are not incompatible. The proof of that can be found in the book of Daniel. In the second chapter Nebuchadnezzar calls all the scientists of the day around him. They may not have had the sophistication of present day scientists but they have at least studied evidence and drawn up theory from the evidence like any modern day scientist. Nebuchadnezzar has had a dream and he demands, on pain of death, that his scientists tell him his dream and its interpretation. In other words, he wanted them to tell him what he had dreamt about without revealing to them any of the details!

They wisely answered, 'There is not a man on earth who can tell the King's matter; therefore no king, lord or ruler has ever asked such a thing of any magician, astrologer or Chaldean and there is no other who can tell it to the King except the gods, whose dwelling is not with flesh.'

They were honest, weren't they? True science only deals with evidence. It's a bit like someone saying, 'Is there anyone for tennis?' and then someone asks, 'Why do human beings play tennis?' You can play a game of tennis according to the rules of tennis but the rules of tennis are not framed to answer the question as to why human beings play it in the first place. Science will tell you why the sky is blue and the grass is green, but it can't tell you why the sky or the grass or even you are here on earth in the first place. Science simply can't answer that moral question. The Bible will, though, for God has intervened in history and revealed the reason why we exist. That revelation is found in the Bible and with all our hearts we believe it to be a divine revelation.

So it was that Daniel is brought before Nebuchadnezzar and in no uncertain terms told him, 'There is a God in heaven who reveals secrets' and God intervened and told Daniel the 'pre-history' of Nebuchadnezzar by revealing what he had dreamed and the dream's interpretation. That's what God can do and the Bible gives us 'pre-history' and the ultimate meaning of life.

Don't you think there is a lot of so-called true science about today and it is not true science? It is, in fact, merely deductionism. Take, for example, Desmond Morris' book 'The Naked Ape', or Richard Dawkins' book 'The Selfish Gene.' Morris's thesis is that man can be regarded as nothing more than one of the apes and Dawkins claims man is a gene machine blindly programmed to preserve its selfish genes.

Now someone may say, 'If that is science I don't want it, it's nasty.' But, it all depends from what standpoint you look at it. It has been pointed out that if you put the human body alongside other pelts, it is only identifiable by its skin or if you look at the human body from the point of view of the gene, you will see that the human body really is out to preserve itself. That's true. Why shouldn't it?

Yet, this is the fallacy of reductionism. The example has been given of a microscope on an ink blob. You could say, 'That's nothing but an ink blob.' If you look at it in a wider context, it is part of a letter of the alphabet, the letter 'e'. If you look at it in an even wider context, that letter 'e' is part of the word 'independence' and that in its wider context is in the middle of an inflammatory article about politics! If one level systematically ignores the other, we will never find the truth.

We must stand up in our day and nail the fallacy that if you describe man as nothing but a mass of molecules or nothing but a population of nerve cells or nothing but a carrier of selfish genes, then you have invalidated other levels of the significance of man! That kind of reductionism is a disgrace to true science.

Science cannot provide an answer to the quest for the meaning of life. Stephen Hawking, the seriously disabled and yet incredibly brilliant and lucid Professor of mathematics at Cambridge University who now holds Sir Issac Newton's chair, said that he sees no need for a personal God but that the universe runs according to the law of physics. He spoke of this on a recent television documentary.

The same documentary showed Professor Hawking's wife claiming that it was her Christian faith which kept her going and helped her to dress, feed and get her husband ready for work! That little cameo was a metaphor of what we are trying to say in this study!

One thing is for sure: Daniel was not anti-science but he is showing the clear distinction between science and revelation. Put in modern parlance it's like a little boy who finds a pocket calculator in a field. He's never seen one before and he starts speculating. 'It's fallen from Mars,' he thinks. 'It's a power-gun,' he muses pointing at this school! On and on he speculates until the man who has invented calculators happens to come strolling by. 'Do you know what it is, sir?' asks the lad. 'Indeed I do,' he replies and reveals it all to the child. So it is that there is a very real difference between science and revelation. No one shows us that more clearly than Daniel.

So, in our study of Daniel chapters one and two, we have seen the importance of the values God would maintain for our aesthetic, intellectual, psychological, physiological and spiritual appetite.

We have seen God's view of science and the true value of His divine revelation. Let's ask Him, by His grace to help us to maintain them. God will hold us accountable for the truth about Himself that we have been exposed to in life. Let's be careful with that truth. Let's stand up for those values.

Dare to be a Daniel?
Dare to stand alone?
Dare to have a purpose firm?
And dare to make it known?

3 VALUES IN WORSHIP

'They shut the road through the woods,
Seventy years ago,
Weather and rain have undone it again,
And now you would never know
There once was a road through the woods.'

Kipling's poem describes perfectly what has happened to a very important question which has been overgrown by ten thousand other issues and which we should all be asking ourselves. The question is, 'Who owns me?' Let's investigate this question in the life story of Daniel. It all has to do with what we worship and the value we put upon worship.

In Daniel chapter three we read of King Nebuchadnezzar who puts up a ninety foot high, nine foot thick statue on the plain of Dura, and calls the 'higher-ups' in his empire to its dedication and commands them and all the people under his rule to bow down and worship it.

It is not very long before certain Chaldeans come forward to the King and declare, 'There are certain Jews who you set over the affairs of the province of Babylon: Shadrach, Meshach and Abed-nego; these men, O King, have not paid due regard to you. They do not serve your gods or worship the gold image which you have set up.' Why did Daniel and his three friends refuse to bow down to Nebuchadnezzar's gold image?

Because although they were prepared to live peaceably and quietly under Nebuchadnezzar's rule, obeying and administrating his laws, they believed they must worship God alone. Nebuchadnezzar is claiming for the state the absolute loyalty which they believed is due only to God. Worship in the ultimate sense means bowing down to ultimate authority. They believed God is that authority and that their loyalty was to him. They believed that God owned them. Do you? Is this a value which you stand up for?

You will remember that when Christ came to Israel He described the situation as being like the figure of a vineyard that God had let out to His husbandmen. They wanted it for themselves and even killed the son of the owner to get it. Notice what Jesus taught them; even if they did kill the owner's son, the owner was not giving up his claim to be the owner of the vineyard. Christ was saying that God is the ultimate owner of this earth and He has refurbishment plans. Notice that when Judas, Christ's disciple, thought he would strike out for himself, betray Christ and with the money he got for his treachery, he would buy and own some land, it led him to indescribable disaster. He forgot who owned the world and with blatant disloyalty to Him. No wonder, the Bible tells us that the field that was bought with his money was turned into a cemetery after his suicide. All attempts to claim ultimate ownership of anything on earth without due reverence for the One who ultimately owns it will end in death, in fact, eternal death.

So it was that when Daniel and his friends wouldn't bow down to Nebuchadnezzar's image, it was not narrow-mindedness that made them do it. It was not sectarianism or racial bigotry, they were striking a blow for true freedom because to be asked to bow down to a government or anything else, other than Almighty God, and worship it and give it ultimate and absolute support, spells a slavery and an indignity that is fearful to contemplate.

All around us in our generation, atheistic and materialistic theories are being taught. If people do not worship God then they must worship something. Standing in Moscow's Red Square many years ago my guide was telling me that there was no God. He only believed in his wife and children and family circle. 'Look, though, what you have put in God's place,' I said as we gazed at the body that they claimed to be the embalmed body of Lenin in the cool mausoleum. Soldiers guarded it. Many millions queued to see it. The Communist structure that my guide had so firmly believed in with all of its atheism has crumbled and Lenin and his co-hort's theories have been discredited, but, what a fearful harvest their poisonous seeds have brought! They engaged the people's loyalty to something which could never take the place of God.

We must never let anyone or anything force us to be disloyal to the One who owns us. We must stand up against it. It was Hitler and his Nazis who tried to take over the loyalty of the churches in Germany. The sad thing was that precious few objected. Listen to Pastor Niemoller: 'In Germany they came first for the Communists and I didn't speak up because I wasn't a Communist. Then they came for the Jews and I didn't speak up because I wasn't a Jew. Then they came for the Trade Unionists and I didn't speak up because I wasn't a Trade Unionist. Then they came for the Catholics and I didn't speak up because I was a Protestant. Then they came for me and by that time no one was left to speak up!'

Christian: if you would be strong when a big thing comes to challenge your loyalty, then be strong in the smaller things and cultivate the habit of regular decisions in the nitty-gritty of life to be loyal to your Saviour.

Was it costly for Shadrach, Meshach and Abed-nego to be loyal to their Lord? It certainly was. They were cast into a burning fiery furnace made hotter than normal to wipe them out. Did they think God would deliver them? 'Our God whom we serve is able to deliver us from the burning fiery furnace,' they said, 'And He will deliver us from your hand, O King, but if not, let it be known to you, O King that we do not serve your gods nor will we worship the gold image which you have set up.'

Notice a fine but very significant detail in this story. The Scripture says that, 'they fell down bound into the midst of the burning fiery furnace'. 'Look,' King Nebuchadnezzar says, 'I see four men walking loose, walking in the midst of the fire and they are not hurt, and the form of the fourth is like the Son of God.' Mark that word 'loose'. The bonds that bound them were loosened by God. It shows very clearly that the trial they went through freed them from the things that would have shackled them by holding a place in their affection and loyalty that only God Himself should hold. As Jim Elliot, the young missionary martyred by the Auca Indians in the 1950's in South America said, 'He is no fool who gives what he cannot keep to gain what he cannot lose.'

Daniel and his friends have taught us an invaluable lesson about what true worship is all about. They certainly became a mirror that reflected the glory of God. They stood up for the true value of worship and may we in our generation stand up for it too.

4. VALUES IN CULTURE

Culture is a very real thing. if you had been born, for example, in the England of Georgian times, you would not have moved very far from the village or town where you had been brought up. A trip abroad would have been a momentous event. In those days communities were closer and information spread very slowly. This affected the culture as it was expressed in art, fashion, architecture, education and social manners.

Nowadays the world has become a neighbourhood and information spreads via satellite and computer link-ups at unprecedented speeds. In the global money market more money changes hands in three minutes than the gross national product of the entire nations! In past times people had time, for example, to contemplate great art. Nowadays they have an attention span of about three minutes as television advertising clearly demonstrates. Everything has speeded up. All of this, of course, affects our culture in its state of manners, tastes and intellectual development.

The Book of Daniel has some very relevant things to say about the whole question of culture. A little concentration will show the teaching to be highly contemporary. We are told in Daniel chapter four that King Nebuchadnezzar has another dream while at rest in his house, while flourishing in his palace.

It is a dream of a great tree flourishing whose 'height reached to the ends of all the earth. Its leaves were lovely, its fruit abundant. And in it was food for all. The beasts of the field found shade under it, the birds of the heavens dwelt in its branches and all flesh was fed from it.' Then in his dream the tree is cut down with an angel saying, 'Leave the stump and roots in the earth ... in the tender grass of the field. Let it be wet with the dew of heaven and let him graze with the beasts on the grass of the earth. Let his heart be changed from that of a man, let him be given the heart of an animal and let seven times pass over him.'

What could it all mean? Daniel is called to interpret and the truth of the dream fills him with dread. God shows him that Nebuchadnezzar is represented in the tree and its stump. Daniel tells Nebuchadnezzar that he is going to 'be with the beasts of the field and they shall make you eat grass like oxen ... they shall wet you with the dew of heaven and seven times shall pass over you till you know the Most High rules in the Kingdom of men.'

It was strong stuff indeed. A year later Nebuchadnezzar is walking about the royal palace of Babylon. It is a very beautiful place. He is feeling very contented with himself saying, 'Is not this great Babylon that

I have built for a royal dwelling by my mighty power and for the honour of my majesty?' While he is still the speaking judgment of God falls on him.

His sanity leaves him and he is driven away from human habitation. He eats grass like oxen, he couldn't care less about his clothes and his hair grows like eagles feathers and his nails like bird's claws.

You might think the story of Nebuchadnezzar weird but a moment's reflection will show that it is anything but weird. It is, in fact, extremely contemporary. The dream that Nebuchadnezzar had just had shows, by the interpretation given to Daniel, that God had by no means judged Nebuchadnezzar for building a beautiful city. Certainly not. God clearly showed that He thought the city was lovely, that people obviously enjoyed it and that it gave them employment. God is not against beauty. Just look around you at the world He has created and you will see that He is into beauty in a big way. Even Solomon in all his glory was not dressed like a little flower of any field that God has created. Any of the fashion houses of the world cannot possibly compete with the beauty of God's couture. God is not a utilitarian, is He? Utilitarianism would teach that a thing is only good to human beings as it is useful to them. If that were so then a present of carrots, potatoes and parsnips would be a better present for your friend in hospital, than flowers! Thank God it is not so. Beautiful things lift the mind just because they are beautiful. Nebuchadnezzar was not judged just because he had built a beautiful city. He was judged because he had not shown mercy to the poor as he built it and because in the midst of all the culture he had created, he had forgotten to give God the glory.

What is the significance of the fact that Nebuchadnezzar began to live like an animal? The answer is that when people forget God, a whole new thing invades their culture. They start living like animals, that is, by brute appetite. Look around you and you will see that love, for example, has been reduced by millions of young people to the level of the animal. Recent studies in the United States of America have shown that schoolboys commonly use the word 'bitch' as a synonym for girls and that schoolgirls use 'dog' for boys. Courtship is dead and in its place is the desire for instant gratification. A popular T-shirt among teenagers says, 'No More Mr. Nice Guy'. The modern culture around us is the culture of immediate gratification. Rapists are getting younger - under 18's commit one in five of all rapes and under 15's commit one in twenty. Sexual attacks by thirteen and fourteen year olds have doubled in the last decade.

Let me quote Kate Muir, a columnist on 'The Times' of London. She says of this present generation of young people that 'Those lacking parents or at least parents who provide a structure with taboos and traditions laid out before them, are now floating in a soup of uncertainty, relying on animal instinct above common sense.' Note that little phrase, 'Relying on animal instinct above common sense.'

It is pure 'Nebuchadnezzar' isn't it? He forgot God and he started to live by animal instinct. So have millions in our culture.

All around us God's Name is taken in vain, that is, used in conversation so as not to mean anything by it. The Scriptures and the values they teach are ignored by millions. The result is a catastrophic break-down of morality and millions of young people are living by animal instinct above God's value system as set out even in the Ten Commandments of the Old Testament. Human life, even amongst young people, has become cheap. Our culture is the culture of the scruffy, the rude, the obscene. In the United Kingdom the 'Spitting Image' TV programme which mocks and jeers at just about everything is extremely popular. Nothing is sacred any more. If it is it will soon be soaked in a spitting image, nationwide.

The Scriptures show that God was very good to Nebuchadnezzar and restored him to sanity. He came to worship the true God and began to live a dignified and noble life. His sinking into animalistic behaviour, though, is an extremely contemporary message. It warns us to worship only God. As Rabbi Hugo Gryn, President of the Reform Synagogues of Great Britain, said recently of his experiences as a child in the Nazi concentration camp at Auchwitz, where the Nazis forgot God and behaved worse than animals. 'All sorts of things happened to my faith during the Holocaust and although I could not have articulated it in this way, there is one thing that I understood very precisely: what happened to us was not because of what God did but what people did after rejecting Him. I witnessed the destruction that follows when men try to turn themselves into gods.' ('A Childhood,' Rabbi Hugo Gryn, The Times Magazine, Sat. July 31, 1993).

So it is that the story of Nebuchadnezzar teaches us that none of us is big enough to be the goal of our own existence. Nebuchadnezzar had boasted as though the source of all the lovely things around him were in himself. He didn't credit God with giving him the gifts that he had. Surely gifts are meant to lead us back to God in gratitude. Whether those gifts be a lovely farm, a university degree, a fine business, a healthy family, a gifted church, or whatever, we must give God the glory for those things that are given to us.

Nebuchadnezzar's story also tells us that we cannot live in God's world and reject God and suppose that mankind is going to retain its dignity, beauty and glory. His story also, thankfully, shows us that when God is given His place in any individual's or nation's life, health, sanity and true beauty return.

5. VALUES IN POLITICS AND PLEASURE

Nothing dominates world headlines in our generation like politics. The rise and fall of governments are meat and drink to the media and every nuance of political life is catalogued. Polls as to government's popularity or otherwise, are taken regularly, long before governments are tested at the ballot box. Conversation everywhere is peppered with views on presidents, prime ministers or members of governments from Bangkok to Washington, from Paris to Tokyo.

God, also, has revealed his view of government and this is highlighted in Daniel chapter 2 and also in chapter 7. In chapter 2 governments are depicted as a beautiful work of art, in the image of man. In chapter 7 there is a very vivid contrast. The very same governments are depicted as ferocious, wild beasts. Are the two views contradictory? Certainly not. You need to get a picture of both if you want to understand what God thinks of government. In Daniel chapter 2, the feet of the image of man is made of iron and clay which simply will not mix. The whole structure proves to be impossible to unite, permanently. In Daniel chapter 7 the governments of the world are likened to beasts and they are put away, not because they are weak but because they are strong and possessed of such frightening power that had God let them go on, they would have destroyed mankind completely and the planet on which we live.

In our generation it is vital that we learn from God's assessment of Gentile government. It is not that God thinks all governments and their politics are useless and downright bad. Who would want to go back to caveman days? Governments like the Roman government built superb roads, the Greeks brought incredible inventions, Napoleon's code is still the basic legal code of France. Other governments have made incredible strides in the whole field of social justice, medicine and health care, aviation development, etc. Yet, in chapter 2 of Daniel God is saying that though governments are often very good, they are all, despite their good qualities, impermanent. The fact is that no matter how great the empire or government, they all come and go. The British Empire, for example, was supposed to last a thousand years but it proved to be one of the shortest in history. God is saying that no political structure is of absolute value. We must not exalt things that are of relative value and treat them as if they were of absolute value. Even democracy with all of its virtues is by no means perfect. Governments are, as the image of Daniel 2, unstable. Why? Because although they are good at making promises, they are not good a keeping them all. They try but there is not one that hasn't failed in this area, whether led by presidents, kings, queens or prime ministers and their cabinets.

Governments, of course, can be extremely wicked. Like ferocious animals, governments under Napoleon, Stalin, Hitler, Pol Pot, Saddam Hussein or whoever, have sought to subjugate people across history. From Argentina to Vietnam, from the Balkans to the ethnic wars of the former Soviet Union, we can see very clearly that government can be indescribably ruthless. Daniel chapter 7 shows very clearly that the Messiah will come one day and remove government and set up His own kingdom. Let us stand up, then, in our generation for the great value of the truth of the return of Christ. Our planet is not going to be left to wreck and ruin or at the ultimate mercy of some maniac of a world leader with his finger on genetic engineering or nuclear warheads. There is coming to this earth the great kingdom of our Lord and Saviour, Jesus Christ. When it comes it will be stable and permanent and will fulfil, to the letter, all the promises made of it. "I was", wrote Daniel, "Watching in the night visions, and behold, one like the Son of Man coming with the clouds of heaven! He came to the Ancient of Days and they brought Him near before Him. Then to Him was given dominion and glory and a kingdom, that all peoples, nations, languages should serve Him. His dominion is an everlasting dominion, which shall not pass away, and His kingdom the one which shall not be destroyed". (Daniel 7: 13-14).

What Daniel saw was no fantasy. It was no fairy story to comfort him in the dark with unrealistic hope. Neither is the value of the truth unreliable, today. Here is our hope! The Lord Jesus is coming again! The message is that we must not debate or dispute its truth. We must believe it and live it and stand fast.

Belshazzar, Nebuchadnezzar's dynastic son, didn't believe a word of it. One night with a thousand of his lords, he displayed what he thought about life's supreme value. He showed to the world around him that he reckoned life's supreme value was having a good time. He knew of God's value system, the evidence had been clear in Nebuchadnezzar's life, but he chose to ignore it. In the midst of a magnificent feast, he made a decision. God and His value system had annoyed him, so, in the midst of his feast he had the sacred Hebrew vessels which Nebuchadnezzar had taken from the temple which had been in Jerusalem brought to the feast and he and his lords, his wives, and his concubines drank from them. It was a blasphemy and he knew it, but so what? Like our generation where the top swear words are "God" and "Christ", he thumbed his nose at God and got on with his riotous party. Who cared? In his view the whole thing was nonsense anyway. Life was a cabaret, old chum, come to the cabaret.

God and His value system aren't nonsense, though, are they? Right in the middle of his party the Eternal broke into time and the fingers of a man's hand wrote upon the plaster of the wall of his banqueting chamber. Belshazzar's countenance changed, his hips were loosened and his knees knocked against each other. Why? Because he couldn't understand the writing. Yes, it was simple enough; it said, "A minor, a minor, a shekel and half a shekel". He had seen those words often, before. In those days they did not have coins for money but weighed out gold and silver on a pair of scales. The phrase was a phrase of weights.

Why, then, was Belshazzar afraid? If a finger of a man's had wrote pounds and pence or dollars and cents or pesetas or ruples on your wall and you had reason to believe it was God's hand that wrote it, would you not be worried? Eventually Daniel was called and the message from God was hauntingly plain. Belshazzar had counted God valueless, now it was God's turn to evaluate him and he was weighed in God's balance and found, wanting. That night a raiding army invaded Babylon and Belshazzar died and his culture, entourage and power were overthrown. The wine was drunk, the crumbs from his table covered the floor, the plates were dirty; the party was all over. Life proved to be no cabaret after all. God and His value system proved to be much more permanent.

It was many years later that God's value system was perfectly described by the Lord Jesus. He told the story of the three lost things; a shepherd who lost a sheep, the lady who lost the coin, the man who lost his son. Now sheep are valuable, and so the shepherd left his ninety-nine safe sheep to find his lost one. Money though is more valuable than sheep

and the lady who lost her coin never stopped until she shad swept out her
house and found it. If sheep are valuable and money is more valuable,
what about an individual? If, on a ship, a cry goes up, "Man overboard",
nobody enquires whether it is a good man or a bad man, a young man or
an old man, a rich man or a poor man. They don't say, "Is he a Labour
Party supporter or a Conservative Party supporter?" "Is he a Democrat or
a Republican?" "Is he a Catholic or a Protestant, a Hindu or a Moslem?"
"Was he in first class or second class?" "Was he a member of the crew?"
Nobody worries, in that moment, about such things. The point is that an
individual is lost and to save that individual, all available equipment is
employed and every conceivable effort exhausted. The loss of a person is
the dizziest pinnacle of tragedy. Truth is, the whole world wouldn't pay
for the value of a soul and it was the Lord Jesus who said, "What shall it
profit a man if he should gain the whole world and lose his own soul?"
The answer is, nothing.

The Lord Jesus shed His precious blood at Calvary in order to pay the
debt of our sin and if we repent towards God and put faith in the Lord
Jesus we can know true salvation and start living for the values that really
last. Never were those values more needed than they are in our society
today.

'Am I a soldier of the cross,
A follower of the Lamb?
And shall I fear to own His cause,
Or blush to speak His Name?'

6. VALUES HAVE CONSEQUENCES

A very sinister element now enters the story of Daniel. As Daniel lives
out his life for God, applying God's value system in his every day work as
a high official in Babylon, some very nasty individuals set to work to

undermine him. Their value system was the law of the jungle where Daniel, they reckoned, was treading on their territory and they wanted rid of him.

"But," says the Scripture, "They could find no charge or fault because he was faithful: nor was there any error of fault found in him". These wicked leaders then decided the only way they could bring any charge against Daniel was to find it against him in the area of his faith. They persuaded the new ruler of Babylon, King Darius, to establish a decree that "Whoever petitions any god or man for thirty-one days, except you, O King, shall be cast into a den of lions". The very sinister sting in the tail came when they declared, "Now O King, establish the decree and sign the writing, so that it cannot be changed, according to the law of the Medes and Persians which does not alter".

We have come a long way in our study from Nebuchadnezzar who, despite his many faults, had respect for other people's faith. Now see a sinister introduction of a written law which bans the worship of anything other than the state and what it dictates. In the English language the little phrase "It's the law of the Medes and Persians" means, to this very day, "It can't be changed".

Later in the book of Daniel we see a power rise which removes Israel's right to daily worship in their temple (See Daniel 8: 9-12) and this has portents of the coming fearful ruler which the world will yet see, the Anti-Christ (see 2 Thessalonians 2: 3-12). Daniel's experience of facing the written law banning him from worshipping the Lord is but a cameo of what is coming upon the world. We see syncretism all around us at the moment. Syncretism teaches that all religions have some essential insight that we all need, whatever we have been brought up in. Syncretism denies that Christ is the exclusive way to God and frowns upon any who claim that he is. Syncretists detest Christ's claim when He said, "I am the way, the truth and the life, no-one comes unto the Father but by Me". (John 14: 6). Soon syncretists will not just frown on people who teach the exclusiveness of Christ as the only Saviour, they will push to legislate against them.

Soon they will not just treat as anti-social Christians who hold to the values of the Saviour as the only Mediator between God and men. (See I Timothy 2: 5). They will see to it that they are treated as law breakers. The Scripture shows that the Anti-Christ, the coming world ruler, will link up the world's religions and the world's politics into one great monolithic structure and any not bowing to the Anti-Christ will be crushed. A huge drive towards political and economic union of states that we see today will eventually involve a religious union as well. Dire will be the consequence for any standing in its way.

Our present freedom to worship in the West is a very precious freedom and we should be grateful to any government that encapsulates that freedom in law. But Scripture shows that such freedom will not always be available.

In his most helpful and inspiring little book, "Time To Wake Up!", (Evangelical Press, Pages 140-141), Leith Samuel lists five aspects which make the Christian faith absolutely unique and Bible believers, who look to the Scripture as their final authority in all matters of belief and practice, desperately need to understand again the value of these aspects of their faith and stand up for them with love, compassion, but determined courage in days when syncretism would seek to swamp them. For many believers who hold to these beliefs and teach them, death is a very real possibility in many parts of the world, even now.

This is particularly true where militant Islam holds sway. Written, constitutional law, like the law of Darius the Mede in Daniel's day, demands it. What are those aspects that are so costly to hold and yet so precious? They are;

"Firstly, the Christian faith is the only faith in the world which offers the individual a direct personal relationship with the Holy, sinless founder of the faith.

Secondly, the Christian faith is the only faith in the world which offers the forgiveness of sins at the expense of the Founder of the faith.

Thirdly, the Christian faith is the only faith in the world which offers eternal life as a free gift now, through the grace of the Founder of the faith.

Fourthly, the Christian faith is the only faith in the world which allows you to bring nothing, nothing but you sins, salvation is entirely undeserved. We have come to God on God's terms, or not at all.

Fifthly, the Christian faith alone clearly shows the futility of standing on tip-toe trying to reach up to God. The Gospel tells us that it was God in His loving kindness and sheer mercy who reached down to us in our guilt and need. (See Ephesians 2: 8-10 and Titus 3: 3-7)."

Daniel, of course, written law or not, refused to stop worshipping the Lord. Note the detail of Scripture. "Now when Daniel knew that the writing was signed, he went home. And in his upper room, with his windows open towards Jerusalem, he knelt down on his knees three times that day, and prayed and gave thanks before his God, as was his custom since early days". Daniel was discovered by his enemies and reported to the King. The King, when he heard about Daniel, "Laboured until the going down of the sun to deliver him" but the written law he had signed couldn't be changed. There was, it seemed, no deliverance. He had signed a law refusing man the right to worship his Creator. Daniel was thrown into the den of lions. As my friend Rowland Pickering once pointed out, "There is a huge difference between a den of lions and a lion's den; one could be empty but the other couldn't!" He is right. Daniel went into the den of lions and that seemed to be the end of that.

But no. The God who made man intervenes in history. He shuts the lions' mouths and reverses the law of the jungle and Daniel is delivered to see the conversion of King Darius himself. (See Daniel 6: 25-27)! It is absolutely thrilling to read the Scriptures and discover that in Christ's coming world kingdom, He, the Messiah, will do the same again.

The Messiah will, in fact, intervene in history once more and defeat the Anti-Christ and all his laws and "Then the kingdom and dominion, and the greatness of the kingdoms under the whole heaven, shall be given to the people, the saints of the Most High. His kingdom is an everlasting kingdom, and all its dominions shall serve and obey Him." (See Daniel 7: 23-27). In that coming kingdom the law of the jungle will be reversed for we read that then, "The wolf also shall dwell with the lamb, the leopard shall lie down with the young goat, the calf and the young lion and the fatling together; and a little child shall lead them. The cow and the bear shall graze; their young ones shall lie down together; and the lion shall eat straw like the ox. The nursing child shall play by the cobra's hole and the weaned child shall put his hand into the viper's den. They shall not hurt or destroy in all my holy mountain, for the earth shall be full of the knowledge of the Lord as the waters cover the sea. And in that day there shall be a Root of Jesse, who shall stand as a banner to the people; for the Gentiles shall seek Him, and His resting place shall be glorious". (Isaiah 11: 6-10). Today we pray that God's Will be done on earth as it is in heaven, then our prayers will be answered.

Values, of course, have consequences. The wicked men in Darius' kingdom who had lived according to the value of the law of the jungle, now died by it. We read that the King gave command and brought those men who had accused Daniel and cast them into the den of lions and "The lions overpowered them and broke all their bones in pieces before they even came to the bottom of the den". The law of the jungle was not changed for those who were determined to live by it. Nor will it ever be.

I remember very well being taken by some Christians to visit the streets of Hollywood, California. Millions of people, I was told, go to Hollywood to try to capture something of what they think is the true magic of fame, fortune and greatness. A more boring place you could not find. In fact the Mayor of Hollywood decided that he would have to create something on the streets of Hollywood to try to make them interesting for the visitors who were pouring into the city. He decided to place metal stars on the pavements encapsulating the names of those people in the United States of America who were deemed to have "made it". I walked on those pavements and studied the names and eventually came to the famous

Chinese theatre outside which many famous film stars had placed an imprint of their hand or feet or foot or arm in wet cement. For fun I placed my foot in the footprints of the famous stars and as I did so, I began to wonder what a true star really was.

The place had no magic for me because my mind suddenly went to the end of the book of Daniel where we read that God spoke to His servant to whom He had taught His value system. God gave Daniel a great vision of future world events and then told him to go back to his work as an outstanding civil servant and promised him a great inheritance after death. Notice that Daniel, believing in the coming Messiah, did not withdraw from life and activity waiting around for the Lord's return. He got on with his work and his belief in God and his value system helped him to be of enormous benefit to the people in the community around him. Yet, God reminded him of what a true star really is. God's beautiful encouraging words to Daniel burned in my mind that night as I stood in Hollywood; "Those who are wise shall shine like the brightness of the firmament, and those who turn many to righteousness like the stars for ever and ever". Wouldn't you like to be that kind of star? I would.

I trust this study of God's value system has helped you to see the fact that God's values are truly permanent and worth living for. I leave with you a personal incident which has long etched itself into my mind. I was driving through Portadown in Northern Ireland one day when I suddenly felt an urge to see a friend who was ill. "Go and see Norman", said a voice within me. "But you may be in the way", said another voice. "I was sick and you visited me", said a scripture tucked away somewhere in the back of my mind. I turned my car on the road and drove to his home. Norman greeted me weeping. "I was just asking God to send you to me", he said. While Norman's good wife got the kettle boiling we overhauled the universe together. "Have you ever thought of the verse, '... and it came to pass?'". asked Norman. "It certainly occurs hundreds of times in the Bible", I answered. "Yes, but have you thought about it?", he asked, insistently. "Fame comes ... to pass. Money comes ... to pass. Suffering

comes ... to pass. Rain comes ... to pass. Sunshine comes ... to pass".
He listed many things in life which come to pass. Then he paused for
breath.

"What about the things that come to stay?", my friend then asked.
Around that crackling Ulster fireside we quietly gathered our little bunch
of everlastings. Forgiveness of sins comes to stay. Salvation comes to
stay. Jesus Christ Himself is the same yesterday, today and for ever. When
He enters a life, He certainly comes to stay.

A few weeks later I preached Norman's text at his graveside. While I
spoke on the theme "... and it came to pass" Norman was enjoying the
indescribable presence of the One whose love will never end and whose
value system is indescribably worth following. May God give us grace in
these crisis days in our world to live for the things which are eternal. May
our lifestyles and our behaviour mirror, in a desperately needy world,
God's value system. As Daniel proved it to be trustworthy, so can we.